The Foraged Home

Photographs by Joanna Maclennan
Text by Oliver Maclennan

WITH OVER 300 PHOTOGRAPHS

Thames & Hudson

Contents

Introduction

Foraging is for anyone, anywhere. It doesn't require
a degree, a style guru or the latest magazines.

Usually, it doesn't even require any money. It's amazing what lies all around us – and what we habitually overlook. Consider the humble stick: if you want something for the home, received wisdom tells us that you need to go to a shop and buy it. If there are curtains that need putting up, it is a fair assumption that you need a curtain rail. After all, they are mass-produced for this very purpose, sold to customers who then take their purchase home and attach it to the wall (with the possible aid of instructions).

If, on the way to the shop, the average person sees a stick lying on the ground, or some bamboo poking out of a skip, it is unlikely to cross his or her mind that such an object would make an excellent substitute for a curtain rail, that not only would it look interesting and add character to a room, but it would also be free.

'I've never used anything else,' says Elvis Robertson (p. 88), whose home in Dorset makes abundant use of foraged twigs and plants. Nature is a common theme, wherever the foragers live: on the coast, in the countryside or in the heart of the city. With the very slightest adjustment, a whole new world can open up, containing within it a near-infinite number of foraging possibilities – and objects. Ironically, these beautiful objects have often been forgotten, or dismissed.

In the former GDR, Auke Dijkstra (p. 118) has rescued a wealth of extraordinary objects from abandoned collapsing factories. Meanwhile, in Denmark, a couple find things at the local dump (p. 64), rediscovering their inherent value, regardless of whether or not a chair leg is missing. If anything, its absence adds to the object's allure.

For many foragers, these imperfections are celebrations of the thing itself, of the stories told through its chips and kinks and scratches. Embracing them is a modest push against consumerism and increasing waste.

The international timber trade, legal and otherwise, is the major cause of deforestation. Of all the world's annual commercially used wood, in 2012 Ikea required an astonishing 1 per cent, a figure totalling 13.6 million cubic metres (17.8 million cubic yards).

As though in response, Paul Tasha's house in Provincetown, Massachusetts (p. 50) is foraged from shipwrecked wood, washed up around Cape Cod. In his – and all foragers' – incredible resourcefulness and creativity, he is reminiscent of Robinson Crusoe (the ur-forager), who, with 'patience and labour' builds a comfortable home. 'It was a great pleasure to me to see all my goods in such order,' Crusoe remarks, having foraged for shelves for his rear cave extension.

As with Crusoe, what is most appealing about foraging is its joyous sense of adventure – of discovery and surprise. Mike Sajnoski relishes Provençal flea markets (p. 134), never knowing what he'll find. In addition to markets, there are features on beachcombing (p. 60), seaweed (p. 38) and forest foraging (p. 198), wreath-making (p. 176), even mudlarking (p. 224). The opportunities for foraging are boundless.

Despite a shared sensibility among all of the foragers here, what stands out most is how different they are – not only in terms of the properties featured (ranging from a shed to a shack to a schoolhouse), but also in what has been created within them, the results unfailingly expressive of the owners.

In each case, and for every reader, foraging is something to be enjoyed, whether it's as simple as picking up a pinecone, or as challenging as flipping a boat. At the end of the day, it is entirely up to you.

COASTAL

Coastal foraging

Coastal regions are inherently rugged and unpredictable places, not only in terms of landscape and weather, but also in the diversity of properties located there. Those in this chapter range from a small shack and a family cabin, right the way to an upturned boat. What they all share, however, and what the coast provides in abundance, are some excellent opportunities for foraging.

The coast can be a multitude of things: rocky or sandy, warm or cold, sheer or gradual – sometimes all at once. It can also be unstable, as along the Dorset coast, which is littered with scree and stone, the erosion of rock caused by wind and rain and over-eager fossil-hunters. By some quirk of geography, the town of Lyme Regis remains safe and sound in its little nook – as do Melanie Molesworth and Julia Bird (Seaweed foraging; p. 38), who can often be found along its beaches and foreshores, putting the huge variety of what they find to elegant and distinctive use.

Common among coastal foragers is a noticeable preponderance of driftwood.

It lines the walls of the unusual holiday home owned by Yves Dussin (Upturned Boat; p.42), much of it foraged and painted with his grandchildren. Another family have gone so far as to make a sculpture with it (Cloudfishing; p. 22), but perhaps it is Paul Tasha (Whale House; p. 50) who takes driftwood to the greatest extreme: the house itself is literally foraged, the wood washed up on the beach from shipwrecks.

In fact, the sea washes up all sorts of interesting objects: shells and pebbles and coral, of course, but also broken-up pieces of boat, crates of fruit and comestibles, rusted old junk. When it comes to the latter, Per Beier and his wife Lotte Hansen love the stuff. Lotte goes beachcombing daily (Beachcombing & driftwood; p. 60), and their home is full of unusual finds, much of it also used in Per's artwork (Island Home; p. 64).

Paradoxically, all of these places boast a uniform impression of stillness – most of the time. Unpredictable they may be, but each is touched by a singular brilliance.

Captains Rest

Lettes Bay, Australia

Two middle-aged men have been out trawling. It's summertime
on the west coast of Tasmania and the sun shines brightly over
Lettes Bay. 'That's trout,' says the older one, gutting the fish
and tossing the innards back into the water, the bay blushing
pink where they land. 'And that's salmon.'

An adolescent shark swims by, swishing its tail through the
shallows. 'I threw him back,' says the man, his face as brown
and weathered as a wooden post. 'You can't eat them, so what's
the point?'

Gulls soon join in, peering over the edge of the jetty, wary of the flapping fins. 'If you want crays, you need to wait for a full moon,' says the man, ankle-deep in the water, unperturbed by gnashing jaws. 'Then you'll get them.'

Fortunately, such bloodshed here is rare. In fact, this area of Tasmania, near the tiny port of Strahan, is one of profound calm and tranquillity – as long as the weather holds up. Its remote location is one of the main reasons designer and stylist Sarah Andrews came here. 'I'd always missed the wilds,' she says, 'the small communities and the peace that is often found among people so close to water.'

Sarah spent much of her twenties sailing around the world, stopping off for longer periods in England, South Africa and Mexico. When her boat sank, she decided the time had finally come to return home: 'I moved back to Australia to start real life again. I had been looking for some way to replace the lifestyle I'd lost, and

then I saw this place advertised in a magazine. I bought it that day over the phone. Thank God I did, because I had no idea what I was in for!'

Looking at it now, there's no inkling of what Sarah was confronted with. 'It was in a worse condition than I expected,' she says. 'I'd figured it was a restore and style project, but the whole thing had to be rebuilt from the stumps up. It was a huge challenge. To give you some idea, the nearest hardware store is an eight-hour round trip. It took a team of us six months to complete, but it was worth it.'

Australia as we know it may have only existed for a few hundred years, but the country takes its heritage seriously. Local guidelines dictate that new shacks must reflect the 'ad-hoc

ABOVE When a space needs something more, Sarah walks outside and finds the perfect branch or rock.
ON P. 15 Friends also find things for her, including a lifebuoy and length of rope.

nature and simple designs' used throughout the bay, while encouraging the use of recycled materials. In essence, this means that much of Sarah's shack was foraged.

'My shack had been badly modernized,' she explains, 'so we took it back to the frame and rebuilt it, using doors and frames salvaged from old buildings and tongue-and-groove panelling on the walls. The windows came from an old hospital in Launceston: we put them in first and built everything else around them.'

The windows elevate the shack to something almost rapturous. Not only do they afford a view of the entire bay, they also let in an enormous amount of light – as well as bearing the brunt of Tasmania's volatile storms. When the wind and rain pick up, it's like being inside a boat, buffeted by the waves. If anything, this makes the shack even cosier, while enhancing the subtle nautical feel that Sarah has so meticulously created.

The 'monkey's fist' is a prime example – not an actual fist, of course, but an old sailor's knot. 'I found this bit of rope at the local rubbish tip on a run one day,' she says. 'Being a sailor, I love old knots. This one doesn't have much use any more, but I couldn't leave it behind.'

Such an approach is not atypical. Many objects have an aged yet spontaneous quality. 'I don't think I'm a normal decorator,' Sarah admits. 'My styling is more like storytelling. When I'm making a space, I'm creating a world. I like timeless things, made by craftsmen. I often find things in recycling centres, and found all of my nautical flags this way.'

OPPOSITE The nautical flags, seen displayed along with a pair of oars, were found dumped at a local recycling centre.

Three mustard-coloured stools neatly demonstrate some of these elements. Sarah loves old velvet and rescues any fabric she sees, often from discarded sofas: 'The velvet came from some Art Deco sofas in a pub. After a good wash, I reupholstered some stools that I'd found on a rubbish tip with it. The local postman, who enjoys woodwork, fixed them up for me.'

Sometimes the collaboration is unasked for – though by no means begrudged. The shack is available to guests when Sarah is on the mainland and several have caught the forager bug and left things behind. 'I love coming back to visit and seeing how the collection has grown,' she says. 'I also like how these things marry with my own found objects, like a chorus of singers, many voices singing the same tune.'

It is early evening. The fishermen are grilling their catch, the shark is long gone, and the still waters glow bright pink from the sun. The gulls, bellies full, preen and squawk beside other resident birds: ducks, white-winged fairy wrens, eastern spinebills. A wallaby makes an appearance before vanishing into the bush. All the while, storm clouds gather in the distance.

Seen through the three large windows in the living area, surrounded by objects found around the bay, the boundary between inside and out appears gossamer-thin. But in truth, there is nowhere else you would rather be when those storm clouds come rolling in.

OPPOSITE The bay is a breeding ground for seahorses. Sarah found one dried up on the seashore, and added it to a wooden bowl in which she keeps random bits and pieces.

Cloudfishing

Devon, UK

The northern coast of Devon can be an extremely treacherous place. Here, between the port town of Bideford and the village of Clovelly, the shoreline is particularly ragged.

'It's called a wave-cut platform,' says Howard, his long hair flapping in the wind. 'In places, it looks like vertebrae sticking up, or the back of a stegosaurus. There are spider crabs and lobsters at low tide. A local guy knows all the lobster holes.'

The sea is calm today. Howard's wife, Laura, and their three children are walking up ahead, the narrow path skirting the edge of the cliff face. The adjoining fields are caked with colour: gorse, hawthorn, cow parsley, buttercups, sea thrift, biting stonecrop, viper's bugloss.

Down below, the beach resembles a roadway, a pale grey ribbon of pebbles and scree running parallel to the platform. As ever in the West Country, the threat of rain is on the horizon. Not so long ago, in fact, a catamaran came seriously unstuck – a not unheard of occurrence round these parts. 'Lots of boats have got scuppered over the years,' says Howard. 'You see engines and shafts almost melted into the beach, because they're so rusted.'

The catamaran was abandoned. Within a week, it had begun to break up. 'We're all conscious of keeping the beach clean,' he adds. 'When the boat crashed, all I did for

two months was collect its debris. And while it's important to remove all the rubbish, I also like coming home with things that might look nice in the cabin.'

The cabin lies about 3 km (2 miles) from the beach, in the family's back garden. 'I carry up bits and pieces,' Howard says, dropping down the steep cliff face. 'It's quite dangerous to leave the debris in the sea, but it's a long walk back – you can't just load these things in a car. It's always an experience taking things home.'

The family forages together. Case in point: Laura is already carrying a piece of driftwood. 'If we say we're going for a walk, the kids aren't overly interested,' she says. 'But if we say we're going to clean the beach and forage, to have a purpose, they really enjoy doing it.'

ABOVE Four wood planks, probably from the side of a clinker boat, hang on the wall; elsewhere is a diesel pump from the scuppered catamaran.

They are not alone: last winter, a load of timber washed up on the beach. This was much more useful than, for example, a flotilla of rubber ducks, and somebody gathered it all up and built a cabin. It boasts its own terrace, with a table and bench; inside, there's room for a camp bed and guests. The interior is decorated with shells, pebbles and dried cuttlefish, while a hammock, made from netting and driftwood, is slung between two large branches.

Elsewhere, a little further on and sheltered by the cliff, is a more rudimentary, though no less charming, 'shipwreck hut' (see p. 29). Built from crates, driftwood, stones and pebbles – all foraged from the beach – this hut is much smaller, fitting perhaps two people inside, and has buoys and netting attached, and its very own, similarly constructed hammock. 'Like something Robinson Crusoe might have made,' Howard observes.

The family's cabin is of a different nature, though its spirit chimes with these two. 'I like it because it's a quiet space, really private,' says Laura. 'There's no pressure from anybody else, no expectations of what it should be, which is very freeing. It links back to that feeling you have when you're a child, making a den for yourself.'

The previous owner had built it from a kit, complete with asphalt shingle. There weren't even any windows. 'As we replaced windows in the house, I would chainsaw holes into the cabin walls and nail the old ones in,' Howard says.

A door was also reused from the house, as was a log burner. The couple replaced the asphalt shingle with cedar wood, its bright orange colour turning silvery over time.

ABOVE AND OPPOSITE Limpet shells picked up from the family's travels on the continent: 'I could tell you exactly which beach they came from,' says Howard.

Outside, along with driftwood and pebbles, is a variety of buoys – yellow fishing buoys; smaller ones that keep the nets afloat; possibly a marker buoy for a cage, the pole suggesting a commercial fishing vessel. There's also lots of rope.

'We collect it and sometimes turn it into usable rope,' says Howard. 'As a family, we'll take a length and try to unpick it, getting one rope out of what looks like a mass of 50.'

Inside, the cabin has a ramshackle cosiness to it. It is a place of both serious pursuits and pleasure – though mostly pleasure. The bunks were inspired by Herbert Ponting's photographs of a Scott expedition to the Antarctic. 'I read and write in here,' Howard explains.

'It's a creative space,' Laura agrees. 'But it's also a changing room and a place to store things. We even had a New Year's Eve meal here.'

The driftwood boat on the wall is a great example of the family's foraging activities.

Over a period of three years, Howard, Laura and the children have collected different pieces of wood, never altering them in any way. The big blue piece – now forming the keel of the boat – turned up earlier this year.

'The seasons bring different coloured wood,' Howard notes, 'presumably because it's come from different boats.'

The perils of the high seas feel far away, hidden from view by the rise of a small hill. Its crest is like a fulcrum, poised between the hazardous beauty of the beach and the warmth and comfort of the cabin. The sea gives back what it takes, and what once was rubbish transforms into treasure.

ABOVE The path drops precipitously down an eroding coastline; the channel was once used for bringing lime in from Wales.

Old Finca Mill

Portinatx, Spain

'I'm a child of foragers,' declares Scarlett Lee Hunter, something of a foraging veteran herself. 'Get a wee convertible is one of my tips. They're like little pick-up trucks.'

Her knowledge is hard-won, having lugged various large finds across Amsterdam (just one of the places she's lived). In fact, foraging has been so integral to her experiences, and successes, that it is difficult to imagine one without the other. 'I come from a family of grafters,' she adds. 'We're all finders and keepers of objects.'

Her father was a photographer, her mother an artist and theatre designer. As a child during the war, her mother made clothes out of old parachutes, a self-sufficiency that never left her. 'Mum's house is a museum of foraged objects,' Scarlett says. 'Everything was found on the street, at a market or in a junk shop. She's got an eagle eye for a find.'

Something she has obviously passed on to her daughter. 'Perhaps it's not surprising that my first home in London was a foraged narrow boat,' Scarlett adds. 'I put her back together myself, and my deep love for foraging and fixing became a way of life. I covered the roof and hull in pot plants, and one day had a nice chat with Paul McCartney when he stopped to admire them.'

From a canal in central London, Scarlett eventually ended up in Holland, via Australia (where she stayed in a four-storey pyramid tree house without walls). It was dance that took her to Amsterdam University of the Arts, where her foraging continued unabated.

'People used to put their unwanted things on the street,' she remembers. 'I still have some objects I found then, including a huge 1960s arc lamp. They were proper foraging heydays.'

Scarlett spent several more years in Amsterdam, at one point setting up a gallery-cum-yoga studio in an old sawdust factory, which she filled with things found on the streets.

'I've learned so much from the Dutch,' she says. 'They're natty designers, and no project is too big. My partner is Dutch and runs an app-development business, while also working as an *aikido* teacher and musician. There's nothing he can't do and he's always calm.'

A profound sense of serenity pervades the couple's 300-year-old Ibizan *finca*, or farmhouse, which they moved into six years ago, along

ABOVE AND OPPOSITE The green bottles and red kitchen stool were found at a flea market.
ON P. 30 The two large granite stones were originally turned by horses to grind almonds for flour.

with their children, their dog, and an increasing number of stray cats. It is a feeling further amplified by the remote location. This stillness is changeable, however, and anything but dull.

'I'm definitely a coastal girl,' says Scarlett. 'We spent many weeks in Cornwall when I was a child and that time was truly formative. I appreciate the verve and aliveness of raw seaside living. It's a very physical experience. So much of what I live now is what I lived then.'

The farmhouse looks out onto the Portinatx lighthouse on the northern coast of the island, and its comforting light sweeps across the bedrooms. The couple own a generous amount of land, some of which is forest, and they have to maintain firebreaks, burning approximately 5 tons of wood over the chilly winter months.

'Regular gales shake the house,' Scarlett explains, 'so the enormous wood-burning stoves are essential.'

The walls are in some parts a metre thick, keeping the family cool during the long, hot summers. 'I love the solid feel of them,' she adds. 'With the wind blowing outside, it's so dramatic.'

A love of drama suggests a love of stories, and indeed, the foraged objects around the house do create their own little conflicts and surprises. In the bathroom, for example, the sink has two differently sized brass garden taps. 'They were just what we had at the time,' says Scarlett. 'They look cheeky and honest to me. There's storytelling simplicity in that.'

To get a sense of the house, Scarlett and her partner had originally kept a minimal amount of furniture. Over time, they brought some favourite items from Holland, including

ABOVE AND OPPOSITE The original wooden mill is still intact, although a roof and walls have since been added.

a tall cupboard with a green interior. A typically Dutch piece, it was once dragged along the streets and canals of Amsterdam, and has moved house with Scarlett at least five times.

'I love having pieces from Amsterdam, England, Australia and India, all together here in Ibiza,' she explains. 'The house is so big, we can really have fun with them. They have the space to coexist.'

Even the house itself has contributed a few objects. The frames with the green bottles were previously mosquito screens. When woodworm got the better of them and they fell down, Scarlett gave them a new lease of life, fancying them as *objets trouvés*.

'The painterly quality spoke to the artist in me,' she says. 'I love random and immediate placement – a certain haphazard, lackadaisical vibe. Too much formality makes me nervous. Simple objects, natural materials – they speak

of history and experience. Foraging, and the subsequent placement of an object, can provide a certain joyful meditation.'

It is a truism that most things worth doing in life require time, effort and hard graft. This often means making sacrifices, or suffering through long stretches of tedium. Foraging is an exception to the rule, and Scarlett and her mother are proof of this. Whether inherited or learned, foraging can indeed become a way of life, but it will never feel like a chore.

OPPOSITE 'When our children were born, we wanted them to grow up wild and free,' Scarlett says, 'among nature and animals and the elements.'

Seaweed foraging

Just east of Lyme Regis, on Dorset's southern shore, the famous cliffs of the Jurassic Coast rise steeply above the bay, their Tetris-like layers of blueish rock gradually giving way to grassy sandstone slopes. The lower, older section yields spectacular fossils: ammonites, crinoids, belemnites, ichthyosaurs. Hunters scour the foreshore, steering clear of the unstable cliff face. From a distance, an observer might appreciate more fully how the ancient rock rises gently from the sea, before surging abruptly upwards.

At certain times of the day, when the tide is out and the sky is still light, a strange phenomenon takes place. The exposed seabed – rutted and pock-marked, covered intermittently with sand and lime-green moss – mirrors the cliffs almost perfectly. It also boasts its own hunters. What they are looking for, however, goes by different, though no less evocative, names: sea lettuce, bladder wrack, false Irish moss, slender wart weed, sugar kelp.

In short, they are foraging for seaweed.

It's mid-morning, and Melanie Molesworth and Julia Bird are picking their way over the slippery rocks, bucket and basket in hand.

'I'm looking for good shapes, good colour,' says Melanie, a stylist who moved to the area around seven years ago. 'It's lovely going to look for seaweeds. You can do it all year round, it's a nice little mission.'

The seaweed is predominately green and brown, resembling a miniature forest. Limpets hang on tight, impervious to human footsteps, while crabs and jellyfish shelter in the pools. It is overcast, but the sea is calm. Seagulls loiter on nearby boulders.

'They've been known to snatch sorbets from unsuspecting tourists,' says Julia, also once a stylist, and now living in Cornwall.

There are signs all along the beachfront warning against feeding the birds, but there is little threat from them now. Seaweed holds no interest. The same might be said of people, too, for whom, if anything, seaweed is considered a nuisance. But if they would only take note, they would realize what a rich and diverse range we have around us. Owing to their cool temperate waters, British and Irish seas contain over 600 species of seaweed. Most of us would be hard-pressed to name five.

'Most of this stuff is wrack,' says Julia.

'She's much better at naming things than I am,' Melanie says.

Julia keeps her eye fixed firmly to the ground. She spots something small and delicate, and washes it in the bucket of fresh water, before adding it to her basket. Normally dark red, it has been bleached raspberry-pink by the sun.

'Dulse,' she says.

According to *Seaweeds of Britain and Ireland* – 'our Bible,' says Melanie – dulse is 'a flat red species growing from a discoid holdfast ... with or without marginal proliferations, with branches that divide in a forked manner'. Aside from that, it's rather beautiful, and will make an excellent addition to the pair's collection.

With around 15 specimens gathered and washed, the two old friends head back to Melanie's house, where they can carry out the next stage of the process: the all-important pressing.

'Julia started before me,' Melanie explains. 'I began when I moved to Lyme Regis. Eventually I had so many, I didn't know what to do with them.'

To begin with, they submerge a piece of paper in a tray of clean water. The first specimen is some sea lettuce, which goes straight into the water, to be arranged on the wet paper with a paintbrush or a pair of tweezers.

'The idea is to make it look natural,' says Melanie. 'Sometimes we clip bits off to get a better shape.'

'It's quite painterly,' says Julia, 'which is nice, because I'm not really an artist.'

Once they are happy with the shape, they gently lift the paper out, shake off any drips, and dab it with a tea towel – or not.

'I don't dab mine,' Julia says.

'Don't you?' asks Melanie. 'Maybe that's why yours always stick so well.'

They agree on the next step, however, which is to place a layer of grease-proof paper straight on top of the seaweed. Then follows two pieces of card to prevent any folds, some outer layers of absorbent newspaper, and plywood either side. This is placed in a press for 24 hours, after which the newspaper is changed, with the process repeated for up to two to three weeks, until the seaweed is dry.

The end result is like a watercolour. At first glance, it doesn't appear quite real. 'You can run your finger over it, it's so fine,' Julia says. 'You have to be careful if it's too dry, as it can split. We keep them in a file, then choose the ones that are good for scanning at a digital printer's. We use the scans for prints, fabric designs, postcards, enamelware jugs. Then we get the originals back and sometimes frame them.'

In the 19th century, the discoveries of fossil collector and paleontologist Mary Anning – also a Lyme Regis resident – helped shape the way we saw the world. The ambitions of Melanie and Julia might not be quite so far-reaching, but they are also, in their own way, looking at nature afresh, teasing out its splendours and complexities. For now, it will remain just the two of them. But who knows? Perhaps one day, seaweed will finally receive its due.

Upturned Boat

Audierne, France

Some years ago, Yves Dussin and his wife Solange were travelling around the States. In San Francisco, they met a man called Adam. 'He didn't believe me when I told him my name,' laughs Yves.

   The man can be forgiven for doubting him. With regard to biblical stories, however, perhaps that of Noah is more apt. For at 73 (a mere whippersnapper, admittedly, compared to Noah's 600-odd years), Yves is how one might imagine Noah to look, were he a French artist living on the coast of Brittany.

Along with his woollen beret, sleeveless cardigan, baggy corduroys, long grey ponytail and plaited beard, there's also the small matter of the boat he's sheltering in – not lost at sea, waiting out the flood, but safely ensconced on dry land: a highly unusual seaside retreat.

You needn't be a sailor to know this boat is not seaworthy. For one thing, it's upside down, with a chimney sticking out of it. For another, it's sealed to a wooden base. There is no concrete floor, however, only wooden slats, so that the boat can be easily moved.

'I can turn and go on the sea,' Yves jokes.

He built the retreat in large part for his grandchildren. Inside and out, there is evidence of their various beachcombing finds: driftwood, shells, tiny crab claws.

'We often travel the waves together and sometimes it rains,' he says. 'It is pleasant to come back here and make hot chocolate or tea, and draw or write about the journey.'

The idea for the boat had been brewing for some time. Yves was first inspired by *David Copperfield*, in which Mr Peggotty and his family live in a converted barge. The image stayed with him, stoked by an abiding passion for the sea, and a love of foreign climes.

One such trip combined the two. Yves and Solange bought a Citroën 2CV and set off on a series of ferry routes from Brittany to Iceland. It was when crossing Shetland that the couple saw a large number of upturned boats, used variously as retreats, workshops and second homes. On their return, Yves did some

research and discovered that Brittany, too, had a tradition of using upturned boats as dwellings. The next logical step was to make his own.

Yves's boat was originally built in 1950, and used for catching crabs near his hometown of Audierne. He found it abandoned in a marina, and only paid to have it towed away. Once in place, the boat was flipped over and supported on stilts. A base was built beneath, and once sealed, the whole thing was covered and waterproofed. From the outside, it looks rather small, but is in fact surprisingly roomy, despite ample furnishings and numerous foraged items.

Most of the space is taken up by a small double bed one end and a table at the other, surrounded by benches. The table was made by Yves's grandfather, a carpenter.

'My sister and I spent much of our youth sitting round it,' he says, pointing at a scuffed leg. 'My mother brushed against it as she sat knitting. The connection with this past gives me great pleasure. Heritage is important.'

He could be referring as easily to the boat as to his ancestry. In the middle of the space is a heater, behind which are rusted tools found by the couple, alongside Viking-style cooking utensils made by a blacksmith. Driftwood lines the white walls, much of it painted with their grandchildren. Another foraged item is a dolphin bone, hung from the ceiling. It all adds up to

ABOVE AND OPPOSITE None of their friends believed that upturned boats could be used as shelters, so the couple self-published a magazine with their pictures.

a snug and intimate space, where Yves and his family will sometimes spend the entire weekend.

This usually happens in the summer, of course. The boat is surrounded by fields and allotments, and situated on a thin strip of green. A dry stone wall, covered in furry blue lichen, separates the garden from the beach. The boat is so near the sea, in fact, that initially there was trouble in getting planning permission. But because it is technically a boat – in spirit, if nothing else – and because, in Yves's words, 'this boat has been along here many, many times in the past', the council thankfully backed down.

On this misty October morning, the boat is an arresting sight. Unseen waves crash against the rocks, dew collects on the grass and cobwebs, and mushrooms have begun to sprout. At the centre of the garden is a stone fire, where Yves is cooking just-caught mackerel. There is a metal anchor and, next to it, some foraged rope and a log, which are laid out in the shape of the anarchy symbol.

This seems apposite. There is a measure of rebellion in what Yves does, although it is of a sort tied, paradoxically, to tradition and heritage – two things that should be enjoyed and passed on, and not left to rot like so much neglected driftwood.

ABOVE AND OPPOSITE Inside, the boat is oddly spacious, and Yves manages to string a hammock across the middle of it when necessary.

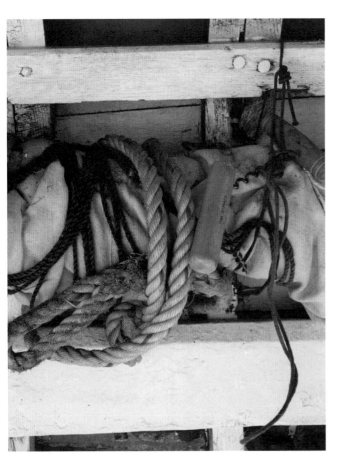

Whale House

Provincetown, USA

The reputation of Provincetown, Massachusetts, far exceeds its size. Aside from its exceptional prettiness, the town is a place of lore and mystique, and the site of the *Mayflower*'s first anchoring point in 1620. It is located on the northern tip of Cape Cod, which spools out from the mainland, encircling the bay like an arm flexing its bicep, or, perhaps more aptly, a fishhook. The *Mayflower* was one of the luckier ones: over the centuries, around these shores and beyond, countless vessels have been lost.

'These people amaze me,' says Paul Tasha, sitting beneath a giant whale bone. 'There would have been horrific storms, men hanging onto masts, people dying in the ocean. The height of human intensity. But they quite casually sailed back and forth from Europe, just like Benjamin Franklin did, with no modern technology. I wouldn't get on that boat!'

While not having experienced a shipwreck first-hand, Paul has seen his fair share of them over the years. 'I dive for lobsters,' he says. 'It's just something I do for money. I like the outdoors – I'm pickled by the sea – but money doesn't make me passionate. It's work.'

It's not only shipwrecks and lobsters he sees: sightings of great white sharks are fairly common in the area. 'I am a little bit scared when visibility is poor, especially getting into summer,' he says. 'There have been 860 pings off Herring Cove, and up to 4,000 in some places.'

ABOVE AND LEFT 'I don't see why we are here, if it isn't to enjoy nature to its fullest extent,' says Paul. 'And not let a single moment get away.'

What he is passionate about, and what is arguably a far safer pursuit, is experiencing beauty in all its myriad forms – not only seeing and feeling it, whenever and wherever possible, but also making it. Paul has been building his 'whale house', on and off, for over 20 years.

Despite its name, the house is not made of whale bones, nor is it shaped like an aquatic mammal. The construction has been carried out entirely by Paul – from the carpentry to the handmade cement – using largely foraged wood found from Race Point down to Truro.

'The outside boards came from some land of mine in New Hampshire,' he explains. 'The floorboards in the living room are from local trees, cut down for development, which I took to a sawmill. I cut the joints with a chainsaw, the rest is from the sea. Each piece of wood is different, and needed to be notched, or shimmed, or whatever. It's pretty level.'

The wood that makes up the house represents just a portion of the total gathered. Much of it has been given away, or else rotted through neglect, as saltwater preserves it for a limited amount of time. For Paul, foraging comes somewhere between work and passion: it is an enjoyable means to an end.

'I tried to make something that pleased me and had strength and beauty,' he says. 'And foraging is fun. Stormy days, blizzards, wrestling some monster beam that was part of a huge wreck or the smallest piece I could get off it. I go out and spend my time in a beautiful place, come home with beautiful pieces of wood, and bust my balls trying to make something.'

OPPOSITE Evidence of naval shipworm can be found in the foraged wood. 'It's really a saltwater clam,' Paul says. 'The shells could be 300 years old, who knows?'

Such intensity of experience and focus inevitably rubs off on the house. Hidden from the road, the building rises into the treetops, where Paul's bedroom is. Inside, it is almost abstract, like a jigsaw puzzle, but not forbiddingly so – in fact, the house is extremely warm and intimate. Perhaps surprisingly, there is no actual view of the sea.

'I spend my day in the sea,' Paul says, matter-of-factly. 'I want anonymity, privacy. I feel better in a tree than anywhere else. When I walk into my living room, it makes me feel pretty good. I come downstairs, the fire is going, its glow on the ceiling. I get a pleasant tingle – evenings especially, when the lights are on, it's a rainy day or spitting snow. It's cosy.'

And there is, of course, the whale bone. 'I sold lobsters to a guy with an eye patch,' he explains. 'I found the bone for his seafood restaurant. Years later, he died and the bone had been neglected, so I took it back. I thought he would want me to do something with it.'

So the bone, like the wood, has a history, though Paul is unlikely to know their provenance. Not that it bothers him: if anything, he seems to revel in the mystery.

'I like how the wood looks,' he says. 'It's more interesting visually to have foraged wood and objects, but I also like how, somewhere in there, are all kinds of stories. The old chipped rib, for instance – I have no idea how old it is or how big the boat was, but I know that it sailed in all weathers, with waves crashing over it. These pieces represent a shipwreck.'

Nearby is a cemetery full of ship captains, with 'Died at Sea' carved onto their gravestones. By salvaging these forgotten pieces of wood, and applying great skill and ingenuity, Paul is both honouring the past and celebrating the present. The result is anything but a wreck.

ABOVE AND OPPOSITE The property is not quite finished. It occupies around two acres, with one corner connected to family land.

Beachcombing & driftwood

For such a tiny island, Samsø, 15 km (9 miles) off the Jutland peninsula, boasts a remarkably diverse landscape – not only moorland, wetland and farmland (predominately rapeseed and wheat), but also woodland, meadows and rolling hills, not to mention picturesque hamlets and villages. Being an island, of course, there is also a great selection of beaches. The west side is more pebbly, perhaps suited to a more contemplative frame of mind. On this particular mid-June morning – as on many other mornings – a wind blows in from Jutland, and clouds bulk out the sky.

'I go to the beach every day,' says Lotte Hansen, who has lived on the island since 2004 (see p. 64). 'It clears my mind. If I don't go, I get a bit grumpy. Which beach I go to depends on the weather and how I feel. I come here when I need to be on my own. When I have thoughts running through my head, I can just let them all go.'

Foraging is Lotte's therapy, and within minutes she is holding a log. 'When it's windy, there's usually some good driftwood, as long as tourists don't pick it up first,' she says. 'I can't explain why I like certain things. I only take things that have a special colour, a mixture of greys and natural colours, perhaps. I might put a plant on it, or something.'

Up and down the beach, not a single soul is in view – which can be just as well. 'Sometimes I sing loudly, or even scream,' Lotte laughs. 'Everyone should try it. If somebody saw me, though, they might think I need help.'

Roughly speaking, Samsø is located in the geographical centre of Denmark, surrounded by the Kattegat, a body of water fed by the North and Baltic seas. As a result, all kinds of curious objects turn up. 'There were crates of avocados and bananas a while ago,' Lotte says. 'Also clothes, shoes and food cans.'

Anomalies aside, Lotte can generally predict what washes up. 'If I go far enough in that direction, I find driftwood,' she says. 'Far enough in the other, iron and bricks. I had a period when I was only looking for rusty iron. We had too much in the end. If you tune in to something you want, you will find it. Sometimes I decide I want wood, for example, or heart-shaped stones, and my pockets will be full by the time I go home. It's amazing.'

The beach runs up to a low, grassy bank, which in turn gives way to wheatfields. Near-golden heads sway ecstatically in the breeze, the rustle of grain sounding like applause. Turbines loom in the distance, supplying energy to the villages. Despite its isolated position, the island has been inhabited for millennia. Proof is found on the beach, in the shape of a Bronze Age well.

'Although it's very close to the sea, it is fresh water,' Lotte says. 'I tried it, but it wasn't great. People believed it had healing properties.'

Did those ancient residents also forage, whether for practical or aesthetic reasons? It is impossible to say, although, in the present day, Lotte certainly enjoys foraging for materials to make things. 'Mobiles from driftwood, small sculptures, things like that,' she says.

She espies a rusty iron bracket. It doesn't budge. A feather is easier quarry. 'Sometimes they have sticky things on them, like oil,' she explains.

Even here, amid the quiet, are reminders of human folly. 'I hate finding plastic,' says Lotte. 'I pick it up and throw it in the bin.'

But there are also reminders of our ingenuity. A rowing boat, long abandoned, nestles in a pocket on the beach: navy-blue exterior, turquoise interior, a smattering of yellow lichen. It is a beautiful object, though perhaps a little heavy to carry.

'Sometimes I wonder why I carry things for such a long time,' says Lotte. 'I have to put them down. But it turns out I'm pretty strong.'

A group of tourists arrive. Lotte takes her cue and departs, driving north past the village of Nordby, towards the absolute tip of Samsø. The beaches here are sandy, and parched yellow hills rise above a turquoise sea. Almost immediately, she spots an object of interest. It is a bent foundational mesh, the squares gummed up with seaweed. She tries to lift it, but the mesh is too big and awkward, and probably wouldn't fit in the car. Walking along the beach, she finds more success with shells. 'I love oyster shells,' she says. 'They have a pinkish colour that I like.'

A scream reaches down from above. It is a bird, and it too is searching. Lotte keeps her head down, either oblivious or indifferent, her worries cast off by the wind.

Island Home

Samsø, Denmark

Sometimes, as in the case of Per Beier, foraging is more of a necessity than a choice. 'I was divorced and arrived at my new flat with nothing,' he says. 'So I went out and started collecting things.'

'He made a really cosy home out of nothing,' adds Lotte (see also p. 60), who met Per shortly afterwards. 'One of our first dates was walking around Aarhus and looking in skips, seeing if we could find something. We walked for several hours around the city and only found one thing – a vase – which we still have.'

The couple, along with their two daughters, have lived on the small island of Samsø since 2004, and in their current house for over 10 years. 'We don't usually keep things,' Lotte explains. 'Sometimes a chair breaks, and that's that. We'll find another one. It's a cycle.'

'We also like to move objects around and change things,' Per adds.

'It's nice to know I can live without this stuff,' Lotte continues. 'I like looking at it and finding it, but I'm not really connected to it.'

The thrill of a new find is obvious. Earlier this morning, she returned home with an old metal window frame, its panes of glass encrusted with dirt. She found it at the dump, where many of their things are foraged.

'It can feel like I'm going to break my ribs when I'm hanging over a container,' she says (helpfully, she is tall). 'Sometimes I sit and wait, seeing what people bring.'

Lotte points out other dump finds, including the turquoise cabinet on the ground floor and a solitary newel post at the bottom of the stairwell. 'I don't find new stuff interesting,' she says. ' It's boring. I don't like perfect things.'

'I don't even like new clothes,' adds Per, who finds most of his wardrobe at flea markets.

'It feels wrong to wear completely new things,' laughs Lotte. 'I get it from my childhood, as well. My mum was like that. Almost everything has been found, or was free. But it also gives me a kick when I find something broken or imperfect and I can see it had a life, that other people used it.'

ABOVE Most of Lotte's finds come from the dump, flea markets or the beach; the wire mesh now serving as a pendant light was found in a skip.

PREVIOUS PAGES The driftwood was found along Samsø's varied coastline.

A pair of old tiny shoes, for example, which are now in a long cabinet in the living room. Lotte rocks the cabinet gently: 'You have to be careful, it's actually quite unstable. But as long as you don't touch it, nothing will happen.'

It is, perhaps, an inevitable consequence of foraging. By definition, many objects will have suffered wear and tear. While these imperfections are often celebrated – as seen in the trio of rusty gears foraged from a beach – they cannot always be accommodated. Lamps are a particular problem. 'There's always something wrong with them,' Lotte explains, spinning round a shade until a hole appears. 'So we just hide the defects.'

Natural objects are different. Outside, a badminton net is supported by two branches foraged from a friend's garden; a table on the upper terrace was made from wood discovered on a beach. The latter became something of a family saga. 'It was a long walk on the beach, and there was no space in the car,' she says.

ABOVE AND LEFT 'I like neutral colours, greys,' Lotte says. 'I don't like screaming colours so much.'

'It stuck out quite a lot, and we had to keep the boot open. The girls were crouched beneath it, with fumes coming into the car.'

Much of the foraging for natural objects is directly related to Per's artwork, which is scattered throughout the house. 'I don't like to buy things for my work,' he says. 'I like not knowing what I'll get. It inspires me. I then spend six months researching the materials.'

Some of these materials include iron and wood, and the finished pieces, which have been subjected to all kinds of experimentation, nicely complement the foraged objects. 'I burn things to see how the colours change,' Per adds. 'The colour and shine depend on the material. You have to listen to them.'

The same might be said about found objects. Lotte doesn't yet know what she will do with the metal window frame, but in the meantime she's listening, waiting for inspiration to strike.

'When I lived in my flat in Aarhus, it was exciting to go out foraging,' Per continues. 'It's more fun to find things than to buy them.'

'If we were rich, would we go out and buy more things?' Lotte muses. 'Maybe, but I don't think it would make us happier.'

'It's a good feeling to find something you like,' Per agrees.

What started as a necessity has evolved into something much more akin to a lifestyle, one which, since the earliest days of their relationship, the couple have shared. Sometimes, foraging can also be a love story.

OPPOSITE When the paint on the walls began to fall off, Per set about revealing what was underneath with the aid of a chisel and hammer, until his fingers went numb.

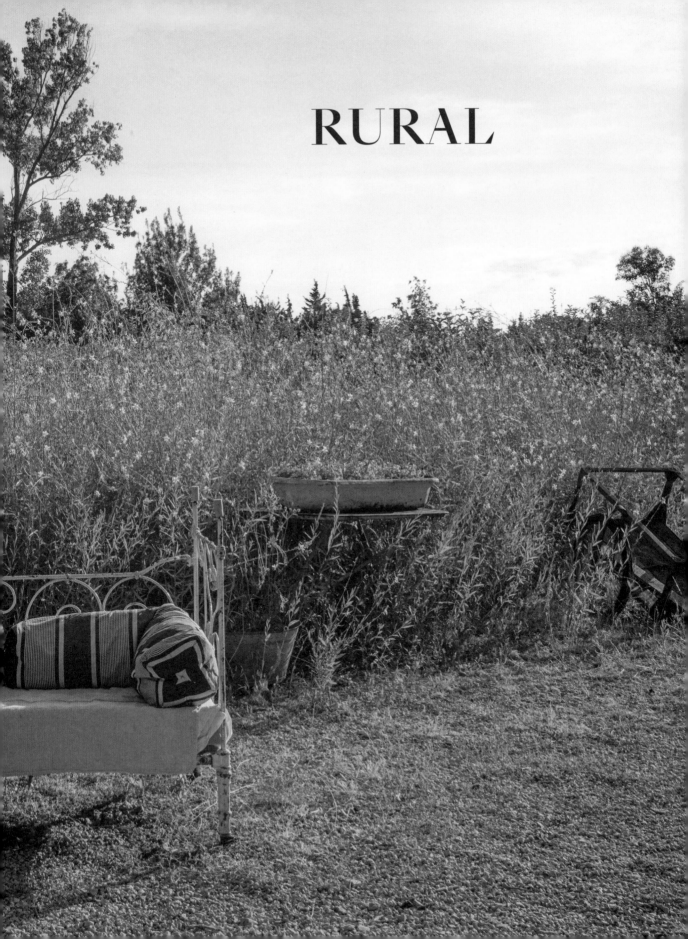

RURAL

Rural foraging

A direct translation of 'forage' is not as simple as you might think. Much like English borrows words like *Schadenfreude* and *Weltanschauung* from the German, so perhaps should the latter appropriate our word 'forage'. In the pretty village of Rensow, Knut Splett-Henning (Old Schoolhouse; p. 78) wrestles with this very problem. The mot juste may presently elude him, but when it comes to their house in Mecklenburg, he and his wife Christina have struck directly at its heart.

In English, somewhat ironically, the root word is of Germanic – and Old French – origin: *fourrage* being a derivative of *fuerre*, meaning 'fodder', or 'straw'. Historically, to forage is to seek or obtain food, which is exactly what Ilona Glastonbury and Marieka Ashmore do (Foraged feast; p. 104). Granted, they have the luxury of the stunning Barossa Valley in South Australia to explore, but nonetheless it is something they are committed to, scouring abandoned orchards for pears and apples and almonds.

The rural environment yields plenty of possibilities for foraging, reaching way beyond mere sustenance. Villages and small towns have some excellent flea markets, especially in France. Mike Sajnoski (Flea markets; p. 134) is a master scavenger, with a raccoon-like ability to locate treasure. Resident in Provence (Mas in Provence; p. 126), he regularly visits the market in Carpentras, one of the best in the area, which sells everything from vintage petrol drums to colourful French shutters.

In and around villages and towns are any number of abandoned buildings and factories. This is especially true of eastern Germany, a legacy of the GDR, which mass-produced fine and timeless objects. Some extraordinary things can be found there, as Auke Dijkstra (Industrial Priest's House; p. 118) proves.

Finally, of course, there's nature – woodlands, meadows, creeks and ravines. It is amazing what you can do with a twig. Elvis Robertson (Cottage in Dorset; p. 88) is something of an expert, and her home is a botanical wonderland, full of dandelions, elderflower and nettles, to name just a few. From feasts to flea markets, or cottages to caravans, the variety is truly remarkable.

Old Schoolhouse

Rensow, Germany

Two hours north of Berlin, in the bucolic village of Rensow,
a peacock calls from afar. It belongs to the local estate, and
struts its stuff near the manor house. After all, when entering
the unassuming grounds, it is the enormous red building
at its centre that immediately catches the eye.

'Most people only notice the manor house,' says Christina
Ahlefeldt-Laurvig, who, with her husband Knut Splett-Henning,
has lived on the estate since 2010.

'The neighbouring buildings had a function, as well,' she adds. 'You need to look after it all.'

One of these outlying buildings was the schoolhouse. 'We thought it was a little pearl,' says Knut – albeit a pearl in need of buffing, or rather, rediscovery.

The 'distressed' look is very popular these days, in homes as well as restaurants, but if you haven't got something to work with, it can come off somewhat phoney. In Christina and Knut's case, there was plenty of available material: linoleum on the floors, plastic windows, thick layers of wallpaper, modern doors, contemporary bathrooms and luminous plastic stars on the ceiling. All of this was ripped out, for practical – as well as aesthetic – reasons.

ABOVE AND LEFT Christina's mother practised *ikebana*, the Japanese art of flower arranging, and something of this aesthetic has rubbed off on her.

'The old and new materials were not working well together,' Knut explains. 'If you cover up a clay wall, it can't breathe. Adding layers of plastic makes it worse, trapping the humidity. There are rules in Germany about energy-efficiency, and people ask if we're allowed to live here. But the house is perfectly well insulated – they had the right knowledge centuries ago.'

Once the couple had stripped the house, they could begin to find a decorative concept – rather than the other way around. 'When we started taking the wallpaper down, we had no idea what we would find,' says Christina. 'We just thought it was too modern, and that we needed to do something. But how much should we do? If you take something down, or paint over something else, there's no going back.'

RIGHT 'If we tried to hide the holes, you would notice them more,' Knut says. 'For the rendering, we took stone from the roof, smashed it, and then soaked it so that it turned into clay.'

As it happened, the walls had a remarkable patina, and much of the decision was made for them. 'We used lime on the walls, preserving the paint that we found,' Knut says.

The structure was also a revelation. 'You can see how they repaired the ceiling,' says Christina, pointing at patches of straw. 'It's amazing to see.'

'The clay for the brick walls is from a nearby pit,' Knut adds. 'The timber for the floorboards probably grew in the forest. Local workers would have built this house – even the slanting of the roof has to do with the local snowfall – so it's nice to see the raw materials.'

Even so, some repairs were necessary. In several rooms, there are floorboards in the ceiling, foraged from the manor house, where they were deemed not good enough to use as flooring. 'It's a quick and easy solution,' Christina says. 'One that fits in with the house.'

The couple have had some help along the way, but it has very much been a team effort – with the occasional assistance of their children. Bendix, their middle child, recently found a bird's nest that had fallen from a tree – a habit he has likely picked up from his mother.

'I often forage for branches,' she explains. ' You can always take natural things outside again; I just borrow them. You don't feel bad, like you do when buying things that come all the way from China and you end up throwing away two months later.'

Plants, however, can be difficult in the house. Their bright green colour doesn't work very well,

ABOVE AND OPPOSITE 'I've never liked cut flowers,' Christina says. 'I'd rather find something in nature that is durable and already dead.' Knut: 'She's very happy when I find dried-out parts of an animal.'

which doesn't bother Christina. If anything, she likes dried plants more, as evidenced by the enormous examples in the bedrooms. The thistle was found by the roadside, while a recent addition was cut down by neighbours.

It is not only plants she finds. 'We go foraging for mushrooms together,' Knut says. 'But while I find lots of mushrooms, Christina fills her basket with tree bark, moss and dead animal parts – along with mushrooms, of course.'

Despite his protestations, Knut also finds himself foraging in nature. 'I was driving through the countryside and there was a piece of limestone lying in a field,' he says. 'I put it in the back of the van, and Christina was delighted with it. It's not normally something I find, but I know the kinds of shapes she likes.'

Knut is better at furniture – and doors. 'I've always gone to flea markets, finding different things,' he explains. 'I might find a factory online and we'll visit it together, or we might drive past a building being torn down and Christina will point it out.'

Outside, in a small, manmade pond, a chorus of frogs falls silent. The peacock's loud, high-pitched cry gradually fades away, and the frogs resume their croaking. Peace and harmony prevail. The old schoolhouse is well looked after.

ABOVE AND OPPOSITE 'Ceramics are more my thing,' says Knut. 'I find most of them at flea markets.'

Cottage in Dorset

Sturminster Marshall, UK

The English county of Dorset boasts some truly wonderful
place names: Muckleford, Tincleton, Puddletown, Minterne Magna,
East Creech, Throop. In the face of such stiff competition,
the village of Sturminster Marshall, located just northwest
of Bournemouth, solidly holds its own.

'It sounds like something from *Midsomer Murders*, doesn't it?'
asks Elvis Robertson. Elvis, too, is a great name.

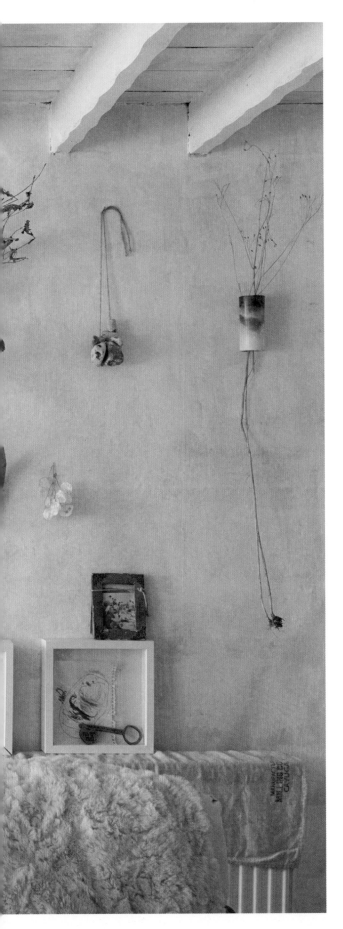

'When I was young, my grandad told me that nature has all the answers,' she remembers. 'He told me to look at all the perfect colour combinations in the natural world.'

Elvis has perhaps taken this advice more literally than her grandfather intended. With regards to her home, 'there were always going to be lots of twigs about', she says, pointing at a wishbone-shaped branch pinching the ceramic head of a vulture.

Foraging began when she was young. Elvis's father would take her shrimping and picking for mushrooms, and she and her sister would go scrumping in the orchards together, then fall asleep in the sun, their bellies full of apples. Later, when she went to art college in London, she would pick cow parsley, drying it and hanging it on the walls.

ABOVE AND LEFT 'The things I'm drawn to are quite rough and ready, so anything immaculate would lose the character,' Elvis says. 'Also, I'm a bit slapdash.'

These days, it's the school run that provides Elvis with opportunities. 'I have a bad habit of keeping my eyes on the verge instead of on the road,' she laughs. 'I know where all the teasel plants – they're lovely dried – and blossoms are.'

The plants are often stuck to the walls with strips of tape. 'Stinging nettles, foxgloves, dandelions, all sorts of things,' she says. 'I rinse them off, hang them on the washing line, dry them and press them. The plants have to be wild and abundant. I'm as respectful as I can be.'

This includes the two enormous branches in the kitchen. Sculptural against the white walls, they have a delicate, ethereal beauty that belies their humble origins. A V-shaped branch by the back door was dragged home after a storm. Not so long ago, somebody doing work on the house said that he couldn't believe Elvis was spending money to look poor.

RIGHT 'I'm a real nature anorak,' Elvis says. 'I can't help bringing these things in.' **ABOVE** Elsewhere, a stick is used as a curtain rail: 'I've never used anything else.'

This is not an uncommon occurrence. Indeed, it strikes at a fundamental misunderstanding of what foraging is. Contemporary aspirations tend to steer us towards bright shiny things, with ever-more sophisticated technologies, producing within us an anxiety to compete. Foraging lies at the opposite end of the spectrum; saving pennies is almost a by-product.

'If you are open to a certain aesthetic, you don't need to spend a lot to make it look good,' Elvis explains. 'A little selfishly, perhaps, it's about what it means to me.'

Having a built-in gallery helps. While the oldest part of the house dates back to the 15th century, with the rest built in the 17th, the gallery is relatively recent. The previous owners had knocked the original floor through, taking out a supporting beam in the process.

'Children from the village perform plays up there in the winter,' Elvis says. 'But we've got it the wrong way round: the audience should be up in the gallery. We get terrible cricked necks.'

Down below, in all seasons, the sitting-room wall is covered with plants and sundry objects. 'People say I'm a minimalist, but I think it's quite busy,' she continues. 'White is helpful to me, otherwise the walls would look too cluttered. When the sun comes through in the evening, it casts a beautiful shadow.'

One object on the wall is an intricately woven corn dolly (Elvis's uncle used to make them). The pagans believed that the corn spirit had nowhere to go after the harvest, so they weaved these dollies as a place for it to reside. 'I would help him weave them,' she says. 'They are a part of my upbringing.'

She has since lost the knack for weaving corn dollies, but the spirit of her childhood, and the infinite splendours of nature, are very much alive and well.

OPPOSITE Elvis added pearls to the stuffed duck. The cob walls are made from horse dung and local grasses, so they are a bit soft and pictures tend to fall off them.

Caravan in Provence

Lacoste, France

For someone with such formidable drive and energy, it is more than a little ironic that Ruth Ribeaucourt's caravan is named after a snail. She searched Le Bon Coin, the French equivalent of Craigslist, and *L'Escargot* was the first one she spotted.

After borrowing a car with a towbar, Ruth and her husband Raphael drove to Nîmes to inspect their purchase. On arrival, they discovered it was near-immaculate inside, boasting many original features, despite multiple trips across Europe.

'It's the Grand Lux version from 1961,' says Ruth, who bought it for €2,500 (£2,245). 'Once I got it home, I felt a moral responsibility to keep as much of the original material as possible.'

Although she had never renovated a caravan before, some things were in desperate need of attention. 'It seemed so simple on YouTube,' she says. 'The floor was quite spongy, so I had to take out the furniture and redo it. The lino had to be replaced, as did the orange piping on the seat covers. Things I kept included a dust pocket, which you can just sweep things into, and the pop-up roof. Otherwise, it was a blank canvas.'

Ruth has since filled it with a plethora of largely foraged objects. 'I've been collecting for six years,' she says, referring to the large amount of textiles not only in her caravan, but also in her adjoining atelier. 'I have a problem.'

LEFT Ruth collects paintings from flea markets. 'I love when you can see fabric or textiles in the background of paintings,' she says. 'It's one of my fetishes.'

Ruth lives in Lacoste, a beautiful village in Provence, and the caravan resides at the end of the garden, where a mulberry tree provides welcome shade. 'I wanted an 18th-century house,' she explains, 'but Raphael wanted to buy land for a new build. We ended up with a 1980s property. I don't call that a compromise!'

Originally from Ireland, Ruth moved to the area with her husband after their first child was born. While spending Christmas with his family, she discovered that they had been making haute-couture ribbons since 1864. The family opened up their archives for her, and Ruth began a journey of discovery that led to quilts and fabrics.

'*Indiennes* arrived down the road in Marseilles,' she says, referring to the handmade block-printed fabrics from India. 'They used natural dyes in the 18th century, and it took two years from order to shipment. Sometimes the ships never made it, but many textiles still ended up within an hour's drive from the city.'

This perhaps explains why so many priceless fabrics are mistreated. 'It's a crime against textiles!' Ruth exclaims. 'I've seen precious quilts used to cover furniture or wrap junk in. But it's also when I get the best deals.'

Common among all foragers is the willingness to dig deep, doggedly persevering until they have found the beauty lurking beneath the surface. Ruth is no exception, and she regularly visits flea markets. 'Fabrics are often patched up with layers, sometimes 15 to 20,' she says. 'You find a loose corner and try to peek between the seams. Sometimes you'll find an incredible old quilt.'

Most sellers at flea markets are savvy when it comes to their wares, and Ruth has much better luck at a *vide grenier* (car-boot sale) or *puce couturière* (a market specializing in sewed items).

ABOVE Antique button boxes from a *puce couturière* sit on a shelf; a 19th-century box of watercolours from Aix is perched by the window.

'The best fabrics come from vendors who don't know their stuff,' she explains. 'At a *puce couturière*, you might have two or three stands with little old ladies selling off their great-grandmothers' textiles. Some of my favourite pieces were found in the most unassuming places. There was a tiny garage sale in Minerve, with a camp bed outside the door. I immediately saw an 18th-century quilt on the ground, in perfect condition, with stuff piled on top of it. The dealer sold it to me for €20 (£18). I waited until I was back in the car, and then let out a scream.'

Ruth is a seller, too, which is one reason she wanted the caravan – 'I wanted to bring my universe to the market, instead of having a boring table with a white parasol' – but she also wanted a space for herself and the children. Even if Raphael were so inclined, he wouldn't be able to fit. 'I'm only 5 ft 1 in. (1.6 m), so the kids and I are the right size for it.'

The children draw and play in there – not unlike their mother. 'It's so peaceful inside the caravan, especially when there's a nice breeze,' she says. 'It's like a cocoon. I'm surrounded by everything that I adore and love. I do work in there, but then I get distracted by, say, the light on my books, and I begin thinking about a nice little Instagram story.'

The books are 18th century, foraged from flea markets (including one on arcane French synonyms), and Ruth admits to not having read them. 'I don't even know if they're collectors' items,' she says. 'I'm more attracted to the flaky paper and marbled covers, or if they are pretty.'

It hardly matters. Whatever she may lack in bibliophile expertise, Ruth more than makes up for in passion and chutzpah.

OPPOSITE 'I'm always fascinated by what dealers keep in their homes,' Ruth says. 'What's so special about the things they don't sell? For me, it's red and blue textiles, dyed with madder root and indigo.'

Foraged feast

Two Australian women wander through the orchards, carrying baskets, into which they occasionally drop some fruit. It is late February, and a greyish sky provides respite from the midday heat. It is unusually humid, and the thick, warm air sits low in the valley, untroubled by nary a breeze. Spreading out in all directions, the evenly spaced trees seem to float above the grass, which is yellow and overgrown, and hang like a mist above the distant vineyard. All around is still and empty, but the women are not alone – and it's certainly not quiet.

Galahs – a common pink-grey cockatoo – swoop down on overburdened branches, snatching greedily at the apples and pears, while smaller birds scavenge from the ground: bright green lorikeets, gorging on fermented fruit, stagger hazily between the trees. There is evidence of kangaroos, but for now they remain hidden in the bush. There is plenty to go around. Each can forage freely, secure in the knowledge that a gun-toting farmer won't chase them off the land.

'I'm allowed to pick on the local farm,' says Marieka Ashmore, biting into a nashi pear. 'They don't use these orchards anymore, and it would just go to waste.'

'Foraging is a deep-seated need in us,' Ilona Glastonbury says, her face smothered by sunglasses. 'That whole hunter-gatherer society. I think we get a kick from foraging because we're hard-wired to. I love it.'

For a vast stretch of human history, we survived by foraging for plants and animals. Agriculture changed everything, and it is now estimated that over the past few hundred years a mere 5 million people have subsisted by foraging. Meanwhile, as populations grow and societies evolve, food production becomes ever more complex – and controversial. As questions arise about supply and demand, with fierce arguments either side touching on the economic, technical and environmental (excess waste being a particularly shameful by-product), for those at home opportunities still remain to be more independent and to live more sustainably. One option is to grow your own food, or to buy organic. Another is to forage.

The Barossa Valley in South Australia is famous for its wine. Increasingly, however, the same can be said for its produce. Ilona's grandparents lived on a farm in the nearby Adelaide Hills, where they grew fruit, vegetables and nuts. They were largely self-sufficient, and Ilona connects foraging – particularly for olives – with her childhood.

'It was very informative for me,' she says. 'My grandparents knew what was growing in all the fields.'

Unsurprisingly, with special regard for the 54 per cent or so of humans currently living in urban areas, a lot of knowledge about what grows where – and how best to find it – has been lost. In addition, of course, not every city-dweller is blessed with large parks and verdant countryside. But foraging can still provide solutions for those in reach of suitable habitats. Besides, in times of peace and plenty, when it's not an absolute necessity to hunt for your own food, foraging can be an awful lot of fun. But deeper than that, it can engender a profound sense of sharing and community, something that is hard to find in the broiling streets of a metropolis.

If already in a rural area, however, the possibilities can be endless – especially if you have an abandoned orchard in your back garden.

Once their baskets are filled, Ilona and Marieka bring them to the makeshift table. It, too, is foraged, comprising three wooden planks and a couple of trestles. Benches and chairs complete the seating arrangements, while also providing extra space for all the food. Local rosé – a Bella Rouge – chills in a green metal container. A zinc ice-box door functions as a tray.

'Everything is locally sourced,' says Marieka.

In addition to the foraged pears and apples, there are roasted aubergines and carrots; dried apricots; almonds; cheese poised, undecided, between liquid and solid; rich, dark honey sliding off a waxy comb; and all manner of pickled delights: onions, beetroot, courgettes, even baby pinecones. As the food is served, freshly baked bread is broken.

'I like community, I like connection,' says Ilona.

A nearby cemetery lends added poignancy to her words. South Australia was founded as a free state in 1836, promising civil liberties and religious tolerance. This attracted a large number of German settlers, who are remembered as pioneers, their strong Teutonic names – Laubsch, Juttner, Eilenberg – carved in stone throughout the area. As a result, tracing lineage is a point of pride here – along with the region's excellent Rieslings – and Ilona's mother is a fifth-generation Barossan. Strictly speaking, Ilona herself was born elsewhere, but has since returned to the valley with her own small family.

A light drizzle starts to fall, but food and wine are consumed regardless. There is no sense of panic or disquiet – quite the opposite, in fact. As proof of this, the phones lie blank and idle. The only chirruping comes from the birds, who maintain a respectful distance. What crumbs fall to the ground will not go to waste; they have only to bide their time. Until then, for all foragers alike, there is no pressing need to hurry.

Artist's Retreat

Noves, France

Noves is a pretty – though by no means exceptional – Provençal village. Medieval streets, pale weathered stone, colourful shutters, eerily beautiful church: not altogether unexpected in the richly historic Bouches-du-Rhône.

Away from the centre, however, the buildings become more modern, fast giving way to arable land, where grapes, cherries and almonds grow. It is here, among the fields and orchards, that something exceptional exists.

Off a narrow country lane, a short gravel track leads to Marc Nucera's garden. Hidden by tall trees, it stretches ahead towards a low stone wall, and, further on, a small wooden cabin with a long, sloping roof. An immediate sense of calm prevails. Everything outside ceases to exist. It is a seductive realm, full of mystery and surprise.

Walking towards the wall, flanked by trees on either side, the garden appears to be one long strip. But upon reaching the circle (built by Marc using stone foraged from a house in the village), it soon becomes clear that this only represents a portion of it.

The garden is made up of several smaller gardens, and includes a tiny *bassin* and plenty of places to sit: different angles yielding different viewpoints. 'It wasn't something I studied,' Marc says. 'It was an organic process, finding the shape and the form.'

The result is a distinct lack of artifice, accomplished through great technical skill. 'I started out as a landscape gardener and learned how to take care of old trees, doing something called the "English cut",' he adds. 'I won a local prize and bought the land with the money.'

Formerly an orchard, the garden had been left to grow wild and thick with brambles. A few old cypresses had survived, along with plums, cherries and apricots, but otherwise the trees were dead. Nearly everything has since been planted by Marc: 'I tried to find a link between the old native trees – and more landscaped features, marrying the different worlds.'

ABOVE AND OPPOSITE Many objects in Marc's house were found at flea markets, including the desk and the 19th-century bed cover.

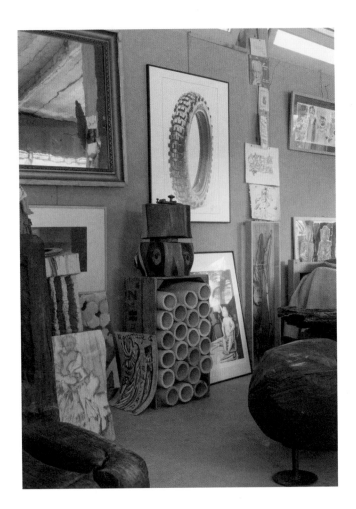

Many of these features are prime examples of Marc's extraordinary artwork, much of which is dotted throughout the garden. Indeed, lucky visitors might witness a man with a chainsaw, sculpting a large piece of wood, arcs of sawdust leaping all around him.

'My father made furniture,' Marc explains. 'He taught me that when you see a dead tree in the open, you don't have to burn the wood. You can give it a new life in a new form. The tree is still noble and precious.'

Marc only uses dead trees, many of which he forages, or has been given by friends and peers. He has to wait for the wood to dry, which, in the grand scheme of things, is not so long. 'The tree might have lived for 300 years,' he says. 'It did all the hard work. There's beauty in what's left, I just have to find it.'

A further challenge is integrating the work into the garden. 'A garden is fragile, it has cycles, and the artwork mirrors this,' he continues.

'It will last a while, but eventually the wood decomposes, going back to the earth.'

Forty per cent of Marc's total output – spanning 30 years – has been lost through this process. 'The role of the artist is to find the connections between humanity and the surrounding environment,' he says.

Examples of this can be seen around the garden. One day, Marc was looking at the curves and spirals of a branch, and decided to implement them into his work. As a result, benches boast their own central twist, with a flat surface either side. It was something of a breakthrough, and his work became increasingly abstract. 'Each piece has its own identity,' he says, 'which keeps it interesting.'

ABOVE AND OPPOSITE 'Objects were made so that you could look at them from 360° and appreciate the craft,' Marc says. 'Nowadays, things often aren't finished where they won't be seen.'

The most recent addition is the sloping roof, which adjoins the cabin. It has no walls, aside from the one provided by the building, and acts like a kind of gallery. Marc built the cabin 15 years ago, using foraged and bought wood. In the summer, he spends most of his nights there.

'At first, I wanted no electricity, so I could live a kind of zen existence,' he says, laughing. 'But I later realized this was stupid.'

The terrace has a few sculptures, mostly metal, including one made out of pesticide spray cans. Inside, Marc created his own *cabinet de curiosité*, surrounding himself with his favourite things – usually objects made by hand, whether by artists or artisans. A good object is timeless, such as the fragment of Roman wall he found.

'My parents lived in a 16th-century house and collected antiques,' he says. 'Once beautiful, always beautiful, so why throw them away?'

It doesn't matter if it is a pinecone found lying on the ground, or a section of tree hewn by a practised hand, the principle is the same. It is about giving objects a new lease of life, and finding fresh and inventive ways to express their inherent beauty. The key difference is that one method requires 30 years of experience, the other none at all.

ABOVE AND OPPOSITE Marc aims to connect everything in the garden, and never works on just one tree. His sculptures require intensive labour: he can't work more than four hours a day with his chainsaw.

Industrial Priest's House

Mecklenburg, Germany

Driving through the green and pleasant countryside of Mecklenburg on a sunny spring day, the roadside dotted with buttercups, poppies and cornflowers, it is hard to believe that this placid pastoral state was once a part of the German Democratic Republic.

Since reunification in 1990, the former East Germany has regularly been portrayed as oppressively grey and drab, so it is surprising to see such colour and vibrancy, which existed then just as it does now.

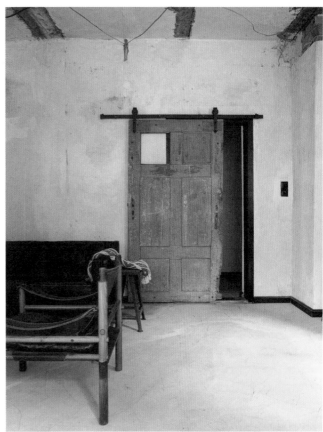

The region's dour reputation stems in part from its long industrial history. Among the many jokes at the GDR's expense is the longstanding notion that their products were shoddily made. In fact, its designs, while simple and utilitarian, had much to recommend them. In a world of mass production and cheap, disposable materials, the objects they produced are appreciated now for their durability and timelessness.

One person who admires these qualities, as well as the objects' inherent functional beauty, is Dutch-born resident Auke Dijkstra. He lives in an old priest's house, surrounded by apple trees and swampland, having moved here three years ago when seeking a natural environment not far from the city. The house is a balance between the organic and the manmade, the lushness

LEFT The pendant light was found in an old industrial building. 'The roof was wide open, and the lamp was swaying in the wind,' Auke says. 'You can see the aluminium is tarnished from all that rain and snow.'

outside contrasting with the raw interior, in which Auke has explored his passion for all things industrial. 'I love old factories,' he says. 'I know it was hard for all the workers – all that steam, steel and noise – but I have a tendency towards rawness, something physical.'

This tendency has existed for as long as he can remember. As a boy, he would flick through his mother's magazines, always looking for the most idiosyncratic home. Foraging, too, began at a young age. Auke would find things on the street in Friesland, getting up early and seeing what people had thrown out. His first industrial piece was a cabinet from an electrical factory. Over the years, his aesthetic has evolved. Since moving to Mecklenburg, where he has easy access to factories, farms and industrial buildings, his style has been taken to an extreme.

'I have done everything myself,' he says. 'I didn't want to make too many compromises. People need a toilet and a sink, after all, so you do have to have certain things.'

Guests often come to stay, struck by the peace and quiet the house engenders – ironic, given the industrial provenance of so many objects. 'I'm trying to create more introspection,' Auke explains. 'Get rid of the TV, go to your inner core and reinvent yourself. We live in a high-speed society, and quietness is a new luxury. For me, foraging is not about having, but about taking the time to do something.'

It is also about connecting with people. Now and again, Auke will see things of interest lying discarded outside someone's home. Instead of driving on past, he knocks on the door and introduces himself. One such object is the sliding door in the main living area. It was attached to a shed that was being torn down, and Auke asked the owners if he could have it.

RIGHT 'Mainstream is boring,' Auke declares. 'Where everybody goes, I don't want to go.'

Among his most impressive pieces is an enormous wooden table, located in the dining area, which came from a long-abandoned factory. 'It was a Russian moped-assembly firm,' Auke explains. 'The roof had collapsed onto the table and rain was pouring down. I had help from a guy with a pick-up truck. I haven't changed anything; I love the irrational pattern of the nuts and bolts. Rational is boring.'

The wood has warped and in places it might serve better as a stepladder than a dining table, but its attraction is obvious. It has indefinable 'soul', something Auke strives to preserve, although he is not averse to adaptation. 'I am a total door fetishist,' he laughs.

So much so that he has used 18th-century doors as head- and footboards in two bedrooms. A 1920s table, salvaged from an industrial building, has also been repurposed as a sink.

'It was broken, covered in mud and had been there for 30 years,' he says. 'Nobody wanted it, but I see it as treasure. People forget that time itself is an artist. I keep doors outside, to let nature do its work.'

Such an unaffected approach is typical of Auke's outlook. The punishing labour of an East German factory worker may have been beyond him, but he has taken the faceless, brutal force of industry and transmuted it into something not only strangely meditative, but also ultimately humane.

OPPOSITE The green side table is from the moped factory, its legs rusted from standing in water for many years. 'I believe in storytelling, always being personal,' Auke says.

Mas in Provence

Provence, France

A long, narrow drive weaves between pear trees, its surface dotted with grey and white pebbles, just like a trail of breadcrumbs. At its end lies a *mas*: a 19th-century farmhouse. Built from local stone, it is a solid-looking house, able to withstand the blustering mistral, while also providing a cool place to shelter, as temperatures here can reach 40° C (104° F). Surrounded by orchards – pear, apple and apricot – the farmhouse squats under a broad blue sky, the horizon broken by a row of tall poplars.

A passionfruit vine sweeps across the front wall and terrace, and cacti cover every surface. It is, in short, a place of enchantment, of fairy tales and phantasmagoria. 'Each object has a story,' explains Mike Sajnoski, an artist who has lived in Provence for over 20 years. 'You can create something magical with that. This isn't possible with Ikea, or any other shop. It's not a story.'

Upstairs, in a tiny hallway between the bedrooms, a magpie perches on a plaster-cast corbel. Despite popular belief, magpies are not proven thieves; rather, they are inquisitive, showing a great interest in objects, shiny or otherwise. Its presence is perhaps symbolic, but it is certainly not alone. In addition to living creatures outside – chickens and a goose, included – there is a flying duck in the kitchen, a pigeon sat on a basket of eggs, and a chick peering out of a wreath, à la James Bond.

'There is a sense of humour in our house,' says Joanna, a photographer from England, now resident in France. 'And no rules.'

'A house is static, but it mustn't be like a prison,' Mike adds. 'You have to find a way to travel and dream within its four walls.'

Joanna points at a cupboard in the kitchen, where two cardboard cut-outs nestle among the crockery. They are figures of antiquity, one standing louche and proud, the other deep in thought. 'It's a game,' Mike says.

A game without rules can be disorientating, but here, there is never any sense of chaos. A sort of dream logic prevails. Anything strange seems perfectly sensible: the mincer churning out diamonds, for example, or the woman in the painting shedding a pearly tear. The presence of a pair of skulls also lends a touch of the gothic.

For Joanna, foraging is very much a family activity, and she has instilled in their daughter Poppy a love and appreciation of nature.

ABOVE A *cabinet de curiosité*, full of finds from flea markets and nature: dried plants, French and Portuguese textiles, and old books.

'Most of the flowers and branches came from near the house,' Joanna says. 'Mike will always find a bin where somebody has left something.'

Mike has indeed found a great deal of objects over the years by employing such unusual methods. 'I bought a flat in Rouen when I was at art school,' he says. 'I had no money left, so I started foraging. One day a month, household items were dumped in the street for collection. I found everything I needed, both old and new.'

Their reasons for foraging are environmental, as well as financial – not to mention the fact that they love doing it and can't imagine an alternative. 'It's an adventure,' Mike says. 'You don't know what you're going to find. It's like a small gift every day, and it's usually free.'

Joanna has always been fascinated by interiors and antiques, and living in France has forever influenced her approach. 'A house talks,' she says. 'We take our time, enjoying the imperfections and often changing things.'

LEFT The couple often find things at the side of the road, including this carpenter's workbench. The green market board was from a building slated for demolition.

Being in the south of France, the couple are blessed with excellent flea markets (see p. 134), where many of their paintings and picture frames have been found. They don't always serve their intended purpose, however: 'Sometimes the backs of pictures are prettier,' Joanna says.

This, too, is indicative of the foraging outlook. Sometimes all that is required is a simple twist of logic, which isn't to say that practical knowledge isn't important. Mike has a knack for finding things, honed over a number of years, but he has also cultivated relationships, particularly with craftsmen and artisans.

'We wanted some shelves for the sitting room, so Mike went to the builders' yard looking for freebies,' Joanna continues.

'If you need a piece of wood, ask a carpenter,' Mike adds. 'A piece of iron, a blacksmith. Just ask a professional, because a small piece is almost useless to them – or go to a scrapyard.'

In 1812, the Brothers Grimm published the fairy tale of Snow White, in which the Wicked Queen addresses a magic mirror, demanding affirmation. In 2017, in the middle of the night, four orphaned kittens knocked a mirror off a table. Fortunately, none were hurt, though the mirror itself had shattered.

'Mike and I spent two days putting it together,' says Joanna. 'We didn't want to waste such a beautiful mirror. I loved it before, but at least it has a story now.'

Which is magic of a different order.

ABOVE AND OPPOSITE The couple are continually playing with the decor, because Joanna is often photographing things. 'The house is a constantly changing beast,' she says.

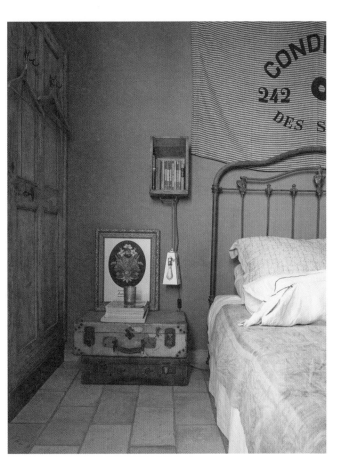

Flea markets

I t's Sunday morning in Carpentras. The weekly *brocante* has just got started, and Mike Sajnoski (see p. 126) is busy casing the joint. 'It's good to get here at the beginning,' he says. 'There's an energy in the air.'

Provence has been subject to some unusually wet weather of late, but this mid-June day is bright and clear. The flea market takes place in a car park lined with plane trees, and the leaves rustle like static in the wind, while church bells ring nearby. Several hundred people wander around: locals, tourists and visitors from afar, in roughly equal measure. Some market sellers are dressed rather glamorously, while others are content with jeans or dungarees. The atmosphere is genial yet pregnant. After all, it is a place of business as well as pleasure.

'I come here every Sunday,' says Mike, who grew up in Rouen, but has lived in the south of France for two decades. 'It's more professional than other markets, with a good mix of things. It's the same sellers in the same places, so you get to know them and they might give you a better price, or perhaps find things for you.'

The sheer variety of objects on offer is mind-boggling. A mere handful includes a cloven hoof transformed into a pen pot, paintings and picture frames, a glockenspiel, textiles and linens, the front grill of a vintage Citroën, a leather cat o' nine tails, old French ceramics, a white column, mirrors and shutters, bell jars, terrifying dolls with their heads and limbs popped off, a bronze propeller, a blue iMac G3, and so on.

The dusty old iMac is selling for €60 (about £54), which seems a little high. However, the majority of objects don't come with a price tag, and Mike derives almost as much enjoyment from haggling as he does from buying. 'I just walk around, look, search under things,' he explains. 'It's a game. You need a good eye to find the good piece. I go round twice, because you can't see everything right away.'

The initial circuit is more deliberate, separating the singular from the mediocre, and seeing how much the seller is asking. Regardless of how interested he is, Mike never shows too much enthusiasm. He can be quite ruthless. Early on, he spots an army canvas bag. He makes an offer that visibly shocks the seller. She declines. Mike moves swiftly on.

'It was too clean,' he says, unfazed. 'There was no story, no character.'

Next, he sees a simple white table, its surface chipped and aged. 'It's not very lovely, but you can see blue under the white. If you clean it a little, you might have a nice patina. It depends if it's a silly price.'

The seller wants €50 (about £45).

'You can buy one for €10 or €20 (£9 or £18),' Mike says, walking away, 'but I'll insult her if I offer that. Maybe I'll come back later. Time might be my friend.'

After inspecting a few more objects, including a box of denim – 'typical workers' clothes, because blue was the least expensive colour' – he makes his first purchase: a stuffed golden pheasant. He picks it from a herd of taxidermy, which also features a stoat and a fox, and a squirrel lying coquettishly on a branch. 'Twenty euros,' he says, tucking the bird under his arm. 'A good price.'

Continuing through the market, Mike and his pheasant draw plenty of attention. At one point, he crosses paths with a German couple carrying a stuffed duck. The wife makes a quacking noise and the birds part ways. Several people express a more serious interest.

'Sometimes I will buy something at the market, and sell it to someone five minutes later for a profit,' says Mike.

After stopping and chatting with a few more sellers, he reaches one of his favourite sections, just round the corner from the war memorial. 'I know the guy,' he says. 'It's a mess, with boxes everywhere, you have to really look inside. It's like a treasure hunt.'

At first glance, there's a bird bath, a broken grandfather clock, a drum, a bottle shaped like the Eiffel Tower, clogs, and a pair of old rifles. Mike jumps in, rummaging through the piles of objects, entirely at ease. He is a true scavenger, picking up and discarding things at a rapid rate, quick to recognize a juicy morsel. He barely stops when someone mistakes him in his dungarees for a market seller. In a matter of minutes, he has gathered together three lamps, their arms attractively rusted, the green metal shades shrouding large new bulbs.

'Only yesterday a friend was asking for three outside lights. Amazing. Sometimes this happens, or when you're really looking for something, you don't see it for an age.'

One gets the impression that Mike doesn't mind. It is the thrill of the unknown that brings him back. He buys all three lights for €150 (£135). Later in the day, when he sees a single lamp of the same design selling for €120 (£108), his delight is obvious.

The first round comes to an end; the second is much more decisive. In quick succession, he buys a magistrate's hat, complete with original box and 'Maison Bosc' costumier label; an enormous wine jar, wrapped in hessian and cork; an old pharmacy bottle; a picture frame and some 18th-century Tibetan prayer parchments.

'A good day,' he says, lugging his finds to the car.

The pheasant nods in agreement.

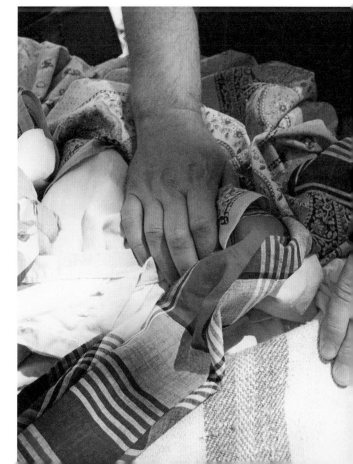

Wild foraging

To be wild is to be free. There is certainly some truth to this statement. Surrounded by a broad and unhindered horizon, with not a single other person in sight, a homeowner can be free of expectations, of a natural desire to conform. This could be the unofficial credo of all foragers featured in this book, but perhaps those in wild and remote places possess the advantage of a marginal head start.

By definition, those foragers in this chapter reside in far-flung locations: on the beach, in the mountains, among the fjords. The homes themselves are equally varied, ranging from a shack to a church to a shed. Half of these are in Australia. This is no great surprise. Once beyond the city limits, a country bigger than the entire continent of Europe, yet bewilderingly much less populated, stretches impossibly far and wide. To Noosa, via Boonah and Hill End, the majesty of the Australian landscape becomes clear – as well as the innovation of its inhabitants.

One of the greatest pleasures of a wild environment is the space in which to roam – and explore. Forests are particular treasure

troves, especially with regards to foraging. It is an unwritten rule among foragers that you don't break off branches or cause any long-term damage, not only for reasons of conservation, but also because there is simply no need. Plenty of objects carpet the ground, ready to be subsumed by the earth or to have their destiny postponed.

Such objects can be sculptural in themselves – Cheryl Carr (Converted Church; p. 142) makes excellent use of Australia's remarkable flora – or else they can be manipulated and remade, expressed as singular works of art. Having served their initial 'purpose', many foraged objects, whether natural or manmade, are dismissed or overlooked. In both of these cases, however, their beauty is rendered visible again.

Wilderness suggests adventure – conflict, surprise and resolution – none of which are lacking in this chapter.

Converted Church

Boonah, Australia

In a bright kitchen in Boonah, a remote town in Queensland that few Australians have heard of, there is a large and varied collection of jars, bowls and plates, not to mention knives, pestles and mortars and chopping boards. In addition to the sheer profusion of crockery and utensils, there is the fact that many, if not all, are secondhand.

'I use all of it,' insists Cheryl Carr. 'I don't like mass-produced things. Older things have more staying power, I find.'

Even the house is technically secondhand. Previously a Lutheran church, built in 1910, the structure was moved 100 km (62 miles) from its original position. 'It was converted in the 1980s,' Cheryl explains. 'When we bought it, the colours were very dated, but we didn't do a great deal apart from painting and gardening.'

The garden is bordered by a large paddock, beyond is rolling green countryside and farmland. 'My husband and I fell in love with the space, the rural scenery, the quiet pace of living,' she says. 'I happened to drive through the area 20 years ago and it reminded me of home in New South Wales. I pulled over on the roadside and took a photo of this old hut with a palm tree. Years later, I would purchase a property next door to that very tree.'

LEFT 'I don't use a lot of colour, and tend to stick to a neutral palette,' Cheryl says. 'Foraged finds go better with neutral colours: it's more natural, and it all blends.'

Along with beautiful scenery and extraordinary starlit skies, the area provides some excellent opportunities for foraging – some more precarious than others. 'Saltbush is a weed that grows in the paddocks and is eaten by cattle,' Cheryl explains. 'The saltbush in my bedroom was from next door. I had to roll underneath a barbed-wire fence to retrieve it, avoiding the bull. I got lots of prickles, but it was worth it.'

Australia is known for its extraordinary wildlife, but in terms of diversity, its plant life is also deserving of attention. It can be just plain weird. The bunya pine has long, narrow branches, with cones that can weigh up to 18 kg (40 lbs). While the trees only fruit every three years or so, the ground is often littered with sharp, woody spirals.

'When you find these bits and pieces, they can just blend into the environment,' says Cheryl. 'But as soon as you bring them indoors, especially against the white, they really stand out. They become sculptural.'

In a sense, these 'bits and pieces' are nature's hand-me-downs, which, while admittedly mass-produced, at least have the virtue of being millions of years old. The asparagus vine draped over an 18th-century bed and the saltbush suspended at the end of a rope are both great examples of Cheryl's approach.

'This saltbush was found in New South Wales,' she says. 'There was much eye-rolling from my husband when I put it in the back of the car, next to his new bike. And asparagus vine is a noxious pest. He had cut it down from the trees and left it on the ground. I saw it a few weeks later and thought it was great stuff.'

It's not only in nature that Cheryl goes foraging. A huge number of objects have been found at fairs, junk shops and flea markets, such as the small stool in the hallway and the

OPPOSITE The drawers were originally from an old mechanic's workshop in Melbourne: 'It's functional and beautiful, from both the back and the front.'

linen off-cuts she uses to make curtains and cushions for the main room. Where once there was a nave, altar and pulpit, there is now a high-ceilinged living area and corner kitchen, flooded with daylight. Despite the church's radical transformation, a trace of its erstwhile spirit remains. When the sun drops and the room turns pink, it becomes once again a calm and meditative space.

Only in this regard, however, does it reflect its previous occupation: there is nothing spare or chilly about Cheryl's home. On the contrary, there is an abundance of warmth and generosity – and objects, including the old brushes, found at a flea market, which fill the shaving cabinet. 'I love brushes and bristles,' she laughs. 'Sometimes I think I was born in another era – these things are very nostalgic for me.'

The same goes for her collections of string and bottles. 'I'm a bit addicted,' she adds, referring to the spools of string used by carpenters and builders. 'I just can't throw

them away. In Australia, they would dump bottles into waterways and creeks, before rubbish collection existed. It became a hobby for people to dig them up. Some were worth a lot of money, but the market has died off a little. There are still a lot of cheaper ones around, but nicely preserved.'

Among the many brushes, spools and jars is a beautifully preserved bird's nest, possibly once the home of a myna bird, and subsequently blown out of a tree. Of course, birds are foragers too, picking up plant matter and myriad other materials, since neglected, and creating something unique from them.

And while Cheryl certainly raids the past for countless forgotten objects, there's nothing secondhand or retrograde about her strikingly original home.

OPPOSITE 'I prefer dead flowers,' Cheryl explains. 'I toss fresh ones over the veranda, and after a couple of weeks, they'll have changed colour, decayed or dried.'

Hill End

Hill End, Australia

The town of Hill End is somewhat unusual. Deep into New South Wales, on the far side of the Blue Mountains, at the end of a long and winding road, it's not the sort of place you just stumble upon. Should you do so, it would be well worth the trip: this former gold-mining town has reinvented itself as a heritage site and artists' retreat, complete with a contemporary museum.

Around February, the sun beats down on the bush, and very few people dare venture outside. At dusk, when the heat has cooled, the town is overrun by kangaroos. And all through the day, regardless of the weather, a yellow canoe gleams, poised, mid-motion, in the dry, wilting grass.

Bill and Genevieve Moseley live towards the outskirts of town, hidden from the roadside by a long row of elm trees. Only the canoe is visible, sat incongruously among the trees. Set back from the road, and approached by a short dirt track, the property comprises several buildings, strewn higgledy-piggledy over an acre of land – an arrangement that has its ups and downs.

'During the winter, the hot air escapes when you leave the kitchen, but then you go out and look at the night sky, and it's all good,' Genevieve says – a great example of the couple's

pragmatic optimism, which has served them well since arriving here in 2005.

Strictly speaking, they don't actually own the house. The property is owned instead by the English Group, which offered them a peppercorn rent in return for restoration work. This, it transpired, was no small feat: the buildings, though standing, were in near-total ruin, with doors lying on the floor, walls held together with ropes and ceilings hanging down.

Bill and Genevieve were tasked with returning the buildings to their original state, so that it was more conservation than restoration – or, as Genevieve puts it, 'like an old woman

ABOVE AND OPPOSITE The bucket on the sitting-room wall was dug up on the property. The old suitcase beneath the table was found by the roadside in Sydney.

who didn't need a personality change, just propping back up in the chair'.

The lease – lasting 40 years – was obtained through National Parks, and it is very likely that without the couple's intervention the property would have fallen down altogether. The walls in the main bedroom, for example, remain cracked and grey, but are now stable, still sealed with rabbit-skin glue.

In addition to the conservation work, Bill and Genevieve redid the gardens and built the studio and bathroom from scratch. This, of course, required planning permission, not to mention the presence of archaeologists. In the process, they discovered some amazing things. 'During the Gold Rush period there were 12 children here,' says Bill, in his habitually calm and measured voice. 'All living in three rooms.'

ABOVE The 'tiles' above the stove were made from broken pieces donated by a friend and bits found on the property. All of the crockery is foraged.

'Taking the floorboards up in the kitchen was like an archaeology dig,' adds Genevieve. 'You could work out how that family lived. There was a pile of sewing needles, and you could imagine the mother sitting there, mending clothes for her brood of children.'

The most remarkable discovery was found stuffed, quite literally, inside the kitchen. Bunged into gaps in the roof to stop drafts were all sorts of children's clothes, most beyond saving. 'You realize how vivid the colours were then,' says Genevieve, indicating a bright blue hem. The couple kept the best bits, framing them in a large box that sits above the fireplace.

Other finds include an old sardine tin, a pair of stirrups, wire fencing, water tanks that now store logs, bullet shells, doors later knocked together to make a dining table, shoes in the chimney (to ward off witches) and a little ceramic pot of Holloway's Ointment, 'for the cure of inveterate ulcers, bad legs, sore breasts, sore heads, gout and rheumatism'.

Foraging is something that the couple have been doing for many years. Leaves and branches from oaks and crabtrees are foraged locally, along with feathers from parrots, magpies and cockatoos. Many objects were gifts, such as the silk spread in the second bedroom.

Because their home is such an eclectic mix, they have little trouble accommodating their finds. The same goes for their many pieces of artwork. 'This is the problem when you are an installation artist,' says Genevieve. 'Where do you put all the work?'

On the walls, in a chair, along the veranda or hanging above the kitchen table – just some of the places Genevieve has found. Perhaps the most spectacular is above the table: a sculpture made of wire mesh and yellow fabric, echoing the dags left dangling from a sheep's behind.

ABOVE The curtain at the window was Genevieve's grandmother's tablecloth. The bathtub was foraged from a house in Sydney that was being renovated.

Bill works with tintype, and a large still life of a jug has been pieced together in the bathroom. He previously ran a vintage ferry from Sydney Harbour and was a boat builder, as well as a skipper. 'Now I'm here, where there's no water,' he says.

As the sun drops below the horizon, the roos come out to graze. A joey, seeking greener pastures, hops awkwardly over the canoe. Neither is stranger than the other. Just like the binoculars and the red Panton chair and the 19th-century wardrobe and the Cockatoo Island cabinet, the joey and the canoe fit seamlessly into the home. Just like Hill End itself, it is a place far greater than the sum of its parts.

RIGHT The rocking chair belonged to Genevieve's great-grandmother. 'I yearn for a set of dining-room chairs that won't fall apart,' she says.

Boat Shed

Noosa, Australia

Lisa Williment, who lives near Noosa, Queensland, with her husband Bruce and their four children, hadn't exactly dreamed of making her home in a shed – not permanently, anyway.

'Our plan was to stay here while we built our house,' she says. 'But a lack of budget and a realization that we weren't in a hurry – or completely happy with taking on a large debt to build our dream home – meant that we've been shed-living for longer than we intended.'

Previously a boat shed, the structure is made out of corrugated iron and is actually quite roomy, not to mention cosy, despite a 6 m (20 ft)-high ceiling. 'I wanted to create a place of beauty for me, my family and friends,' Lisa says, 'where we could all feel relaxed and cherished.'

Three large yachts had been built in the shed, evidence of which include a pedal toilet and a ladder leading up to the loft bedroom. There are also lots of trees out front, including gum, fig, silky oak and lychee. In order to see them, and to let in some sunlight, the family must open the front doors, owing to the small number of (salvaged) windows.

Surprisingly, the result is not at all gloomy: a large dining and sitting area dominates the shed, with bedrooms partitioned off to the side, and a play area and kitchen at the back. It is

ABOVE AND OPPOSITE 'The one constant thing in my life has always been making things look nice,' Lisa says. 'I find true beauty in the frayed and worn.'

also an excellent excuse to sit in the garden, sometimes in 'Fred's Seat', which Bruce made in honour of the shed's previous owner, whose ashes were scattered nearby.

'The more time I spend living in this space, the more I admire the ruggedness, the roughness and the challenges,' Lisa says. 'It has become our family home.'

While some things in life don't always go to plan, others can appear predestined. As a young child on holiday with her family in the Sunshine Coast Hinterland, Lisa turned to her mother and declared that one day she would get married there. 'And that's exactly what I did!' she laughs. 'The greenness had captivated me and the affinity I felt with the trees has never left me.'

And, indeed, she has never left the trees. 'Foraging in nature grounds me,' she continues. 'It's a necessity. Nature creates and offers such beauty for us to admire. By bringing this into our home, I feel deeply connected and grateful. It's the most beautiful work of art available.'

Branches hang from the walls and doors, along with wattle and banksia flowers and seed pods, all of which are suitable for drying. In one corner, Lisa has constructed a 'foraged foliage' wall, which consists of once-fresh flowers given for birthdays and anniversaries.

'They are left to dry, creating a carpet of loveliness,' she says. 'I actually spend much of my time making natural dye pots using found leaves, flowers, seeds and pods, with which I dye anything that is less than new. Natural fibres take the colours beautifully.'

For as long as Lisa can remember, she has always been a forager. It wasn't something she inherited, however: 'I come from a very organized, tidy, don't-scratch-anything upbringing. My way was a worry to my parents. They are English and grew up

OPPOSITE The dining table was a wedding present, made from old pine floorboards that have become further weathered and marked over the past 24 years.

during the war, so they didn't have the luxury to choose between new or worn. They couldn't understand why I would want to surround myself with old, beaten-up things.'

Lisa recalls one of her earlier works causing great consternation: 'I bought an old washing trolley and a bentwood chair with a broken leg. I displayed the pieces in a corner of my bedroom with a large pot plant coming through the broken seat. My father abhorred it! From that day onward, my bedroom door was always shut so that the shameful sight couldn't be seen.'

Since those youthful experiments, nearly all of Lisa's furniture has been salvaged, reclaimed or built from scratch (the work bench in the play area, for example, was made by Bruce using foraged timber). The couple find lots of pieces in secondhand shops, while others are handed down from family and friends who want something new.

The roadside is another excellent repository. 'One of our most impressive finds is our piano,

which was discarded and sitting in an old shed,' she says. 'We've done some research, and found that it's around 120 years old. It travelled from South Africa, and it is amazing to think of the journey it has taken to find itself here.'

For Lisa, it is as much about the history of the piece as it is about its beauty and age. 'I love the thought that it has been a part of someone else's life story. That every mark, dint, scuff or mend has been due to an event, a moment in someone else's life. I relish that thought, and like to think I add to the next part of the story.'

It is the very least she does.

ABOVE AND OPPOSITE The shed is nestled among lush green hills, ancient creeks and amazing birdlife: 'It is exactly what I would have wished for as that little girl on those family picnics.'

Dune Shack

Provincetown, USA

Dune Shack in Provincetown can only be reached on foot –
a blessing, of a sort, if what you are seeking is solitude. Many have
done so over the years, including American literary and artistic
heavyweights such as Jackson Pollock, Mark Rothko and Norman
Mailer. But the most famous resident – as far as the locals are
concerned – was Harry Kemp, the so-called 'poet of the dunes',
who died in 1960.

'I really feel his presence here,' says Anie Stanley, a multimedia artist and native New Yorker. Together with Juliette Hermant, a French-born artist and entrepreneur, she 'rents' Harry Kemp's old dune shack on Cape Cod from Paul Tasha (see p. 50).

The number of dune shacks in the Peaked Hill Bar Historic District totals 19, each built from foraged wood, washed up on the shoreline. During the 1960s, the residents were gradually pushed out as the area became protected. Since the mid-1990s, however, the National Park Service has agreed to let non-profit organizations offer artist-in-residence programmes.

It was Anie who introduced Juliette to the area. 'I first came to Provincetown in the 1980s and met Paul's mum Sunny, who told us about

LEFT 'It's great to have a secluded moment,' Anie says. 'Hearing the ocean at night, and falling asleep to the crashing of the waves.'

the shack,' she says. 'A friend and I hiked out there, arriving in the evening with snacks and a bottle of wine, and we had to spend the night. Years later, Juliette and I went with supplies, wine, canvases, a camera, and stayed for three nights. We couldn't stop thinking about it.'

There are three dominant features beyond the shack: the sea, the sky and the dunes. In between are cliffs, rosehip bushes, trees, grasses and wildlife. Juliette makes jelly from the rosehips, and she and Anie regularly forage wood for the fire pit. 'I built Juliette an easel with wood found on the beach,' Anie remembers. 'Obviously, it got blown away.'

The shack has barely been touched – and Anie should know. She uses a lot of reclaimed wood and materials in her design projects. 'You can tell they had to do some repairs over the years, but it is the same now as it was in 1988, apart from a missing window pane,' she says. 'A very simple design, no frills, all foraged wood and salvaged windows.'

'We're breathing a little life into it,' Juliette adds, 'bringing in some flowers from outside, or things picked up from the beach, like small rocks and oyster shells and driftwood.'

Oddly enough, it had long been a dream of Juliette's to live in an isolated structure with a history. 'I remember opening the door and seeing the bareness, just a little kitchenette and an area for tools,' she says. 'I just loved it. I'm attracted to what has already been made: I'm a professional decorator who doesn't decorate.'

In a remote place such as this, the rhythms of the day affect the body and the mind. 'I've just turned 50, and I was 19 when I stayed here for the first time,' Anie says. 'I wrote poetry back then, and I'm now feeling that call to write again. It must be for a reason.'

ABOVE 'Wherever I have lived in the world, foraging is a way of grounding myself, of being present,' says Juliette. 'It is a way of observing what's around me.'

Wreath-making
& floral sculptures

Over the course of history, wreaths have come to symbolize many different things: in Greco-Roman society, occupation, rank and status; in ancient Egypt, victory over death; in modern times, an expression of sorrow; at Christmas, growth and everlasting life. While the meanings differ, they all share a similar form: that of a circle, or near enough, the root words of 'wreath' translated as 'twist' or 'a thing bound around'. They also share a suggestion of continuity and endurance – ideas that, consciously or otherwise, both Kate Brew and Tracey Deep play with.

Tracey lives in Sydney; Kate in the Adelaide Hills. The only things connecting them are a shared nationality and their nuanced approaches to wreath-making, not to mention a love of foraging and the way it informs their respective work. Where others have used palm, holly and laurel, Kate and Tracey employ found objects of a more idiosyncratic nature.

Kate began foraging in Cudlee Creek, a small town northeast of Adelaide. 'We didn't have a lot of money,' she explains, 'and finding things from outside instantly made me feel better.'

Initially foraging for the home, Kate soon started making things of her own. 'In the street we lived there were three pieces of wire an inch thick, and they were slung over an old post,' she remembers. 'The wire looked great on the wall. I then started pulling down old woody vines, twisting them into new shapes.'

Tracey, meanwhile, has always had a passion for collecting, intrigued as a child by things she found, either at the beach, in the park or on the streets. 'I started creating things with Australian native plants – banksia and eucalyptus, for example,' she says, 'using flowers and seed pods and things I would usually find on walks, often rescuing them after a storm. I collected anything from nature that was textural and interesting. After a number of years, it evolved into making sculptural artworks.'

Tracey works in Redfern, an inner-city suburb on the rise. The building itself is oddly nondescript, the upper floors occupied by offices, the main hallway somewhat dreary. This only heightens the impact of her studio, its presence signalled by a sweetly pervasive scent. 'I collect and collect,' she says. 'It's a bit of a wonderland in here.'

In a relatively small space – its dimensions impossible to determine, owing to a profusion of towering plantlife – Tracey has room for a table, a radio and not much else. Nonetheless, she has managed to carve a winding path through all the foliage, enabling her to gain access when required. 'The material forms the idea,' she says. 'I'll play with it for a while and see what works. When I find something, it will sit for a while until an idea unfolds. There is nothing more exciting than playing with something new that you've found.'

Kate works from home – a sprawling erstwhile dairy farm, set among gloriously verdant hills, the property adjoined by a kangaroo sanctuary. 'I studied art and textiles when crafts were becoming unfashionable,' she says. 'There's a resurgence now.'

There is something joyously spontaneous about her wreaths, which she makes out of whatever materials she can find: rusted wire, silver birch, wattle wood and grasses, a bamboo husk, sheep bones. 'With silver birch, the technique is to weave the material back in on itself, so that it holds its form,' she explains. 'When I make things, I try not to intervene with them too much. I like to be able to keep them in their raw state.'

There is a piece hanging on the wall of the old creamery. It is burnt and bent out of shape. 'I found some wire, made it, hated it, threw it on the bonfire, then saw it weeks later and liked it,' Kate remembers. 'It had created its own little story.'

Stories are equally important to Tracey. 'I'm inspired by found things,' she says. 'When people throw out plants, it breaks my heart. There is history in these plants and I find them just as beautiful in their afterlife. I want to transform them into something new that others will also find beautiful.'

Unless they are woody, plants tend to disintegrate. As a result, Tracey's flower-based artworks are, as she says, 'semi-permanent', while found objects form the basis of her permanent ones. 'I love it when Aussie flora goes into the next phase, and the petals start to crumble,' she says. 'One flower has golden blooms that slowly disappear, leaving these stalks that look like coral. I find this a lot with native plants. They tend to look like something from under the sea.'

Tracey has also been known to use fishing nets, foraged directly from the docks. 'Nature is food for the soul for me,' she says. 'They are trying to stop these fine nets because of the marine life that get caught in them. When I work with them, I feel what those creatures must feel, because I get knotted and twisted in them all the time. It looks fragile, but it's quite ferocious to work with.'

Similar perhaps in spirit, Kate's motivations spring from something different. 'A few years ago a bushfire swept through the Adelaide Hills,' she says. 'We had four children at the time, and, after saying goodbye to the emu and the sheep, we filled two cars with our things. It was weird to pack your life into such a small space. Fortunately, the house was fine, but it was a wake-up call to embrace the moment.'

By using foraged objects – some durable, some ephemeral – both Kate and Tracey give renewed depth and meaning to what in effect has become invisible. Against all odds, the objects endure, if sometimes only briefly.

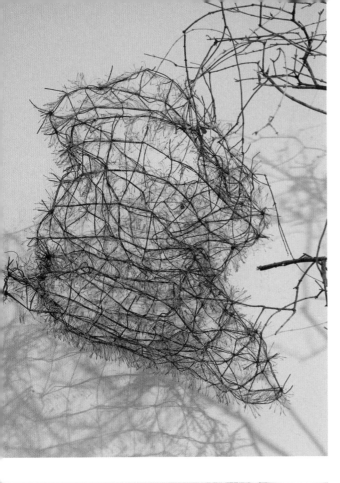

Woodsman's Hut

Western Fjords, Norway

Heidi Bjørnsdotter Thorvik picks her way through the forest.
The ground is dense and mossy, and the narrow path is dotted
with stones, each one placed by a family member, going back many
years. As she walks, she eats foraged blueberries and cranberries,
a knife and scabbard secured to her belt.

'It is an old custom, but not used in Norway so much anymore,'
Heidi says of her middle name. 'It literally means "Bjørn's daughter".'

This neatly summarizes two important aspects of her – and her family's – life: tradition, and her father. 'My father's name is Bjørn Sandvik,' she says. 'He was born in 1945 and grew up on a timber farm in the middle of nowhere, surrounded by forest, close to the sea. There was only a small road for horses and he had to walk or take a boat to school.'

It is mid-August among Norway's southwestern fjords, not far from the town of Stavanger, and the weather alternates between sun, rain and cloud. The stillness of the forest is almost absolute.

'My father is a quiet man,' Heidi continues. 'In nature, especially, he's a listener. He didn't like it when my siblings and I would scream. He wanted us to listen to the birds and other

ABOVE AND LEFT Fresh water is available from the lake. Heidi's father restored the rowing boat, and there's also a lakeside fire pit, plus benches and a bathing area.

animals, even the whispering of the grass and trees. He feels very alive here. The cabins are his escape, a place of peace and tranquillity.'

Heidi emerges from the forest, straight into a clearing with a lake. Its surface is peppered with water lilies, and rocky hills rise up either side. Two wooden cabins sit on a grassy promontory, each on a stone foundation.

'The stones come from nearby,' she explains. 'My father made a zip-line to carry them 100 m (328 ft) down the hill. The wood came from the forest and elsewhere in the area. You can't just use any kind of wood: the shape is vital.'

The cabins have stood as they are now since 2000. The smaller one was built from scratch by Bjørn, while the larger one, now used as a workshop and for storing chopped wood, was built by Heidi's grandfather in the 1940s.

'It was only meant to last 10 years,' she says. 'It was slowly rotting, but my father saved the good materials and moved it further down. It's very similar to the original.'

Her grandfather owned and ran the timber farm. During the winter, he would chop down the trees and transport them to the farm with a horse and sleigh. 'Modern machines can do in a day what took him the entire winter,' Heidi muses.

He built the cabin to sleep in if the working day was long. Bjørn was taken there as a child and would help with the work. He fell in love with the place and became a builder by trade, restoring old buildings using traditional techniques, becoming an expert on the forest and advising local farmers on their woodlands.

Such skills are evident in the construction of the cabins. In addition to the use of local trees, each cabin boasts a *taktorv*, or turf roof. 'It goes back to the Vikings and even earlier,' Heidi says. 'It's about using available materials.'

ABOVE The hooks on the wall are made from a common bush found in the area, a traditional use that also extends to sculptures and small tools.

The first layer of the sloping roof is wood, which can be seen from the inside. On top of this is a layer of birch bark, which is waterproof, followed by tight clumps of turf. Grasses and flowers grow on top, broken by a chimney on the smaller cabin. The same goes for the toilet, which leans against a rocky outcrop and has no door, affording incredible views of the forest. 'Watch out for the toad,' Heidi jokes.

The cabins are filled with several foraged objects. Most arresting, perhaps, are the wooden bowls and cups. They are made from cankers, which are naturally circular, not to mention extremely hardy. 'You can cut these things right off the trees,' she says.

When Heidi and her siblings were children, their father was always chopping something, finding weird branches, or collecting stones, wasp's and bird's nests. It is something that has inspired all of his children, and now Heidi regularly forages in Oslo (see p. 198), where she lives with her husband and two sons.

'We all have a close relationship with this place, my brother and sisters and all of our children. I remember my grandmother baking bread and I can still smell the peanut butter in the cabin. I get really emotional about peanut butter, it's a family joke. When we were younger, of course, we would bring our girlfriends and boyfriends here. It's very romantic.'

Heidi's father is now one of the oldest members of the family, and she worries that his knowledge and skills will die with him. Even if that's true, his legacy will certainly live on, and future generations will doubtless fall as much in love with the forest as he once did.

ABOVE AND OPPOSITE There's nobody else around – a rare commodity these days. It's an important place for the family, and everyone was taken here as a baby.

Village House

Mindya, Bulgaria

One of the first things you notice is the bees. If coming from England, or any other developed and densely populated country, the volume of their buzzing can be shocking.

Mindya – a village nestled in the foothills of the Balkans, in central Bulgaria – is somewhat isolated, located roughly three hours from Sofia. It is also very beautiful, the landscape thick with trees and flowers, while the village itself has an easy, dishevelled charm, although one that is touched by melancholy.

The streets are littered with rundown or abandoned buildings, a result of the newish bypass. Even so, there is plenty of colour, not only on the walls of the houses, but also in the surrounding meadows and fields. Most villagers can't afford pesticides, and so everything here is organic – hence the heavy bee traffic.

'It was the cheapest place in Europe to buy property,' says Tim Clinch, a professional photographer, who has previously lived in London, France and Spain. 'I got divorced and lost everything, which isn't necessarily a bad thing. My partner suggested looking in Bulgaria. It was the first house we saw, although we looked at 40 or more. The view was perfect, and the house cost less than a secondhand family car. Although I was unconvinced at first, I soon fell in love with both the house and the country.'

ABOVE A Bulgarian vase from the 1970s sits atop an old painted chest. **ON P. 190** The balcony contains flea-market finds from the village of Gorna Oryahovitsa.

Tim has tried to retain as much of the original building as possible, leaving the exterior almost exactly as they found it. The interior is predominately red, white and green – the colours of the Bulgarian flag – and the couple have refrained from modernizing too much, for fear of losing the traditional 'feel' of the house – something the previous owners appreciate when they occasionally pop round.

'They come round every year to attach a necrologue,' explains Tim. 'It's a strange, rather charming tradition. On the anniversary of a death, they hang a picture and a short biography of the deceased on the house. It sounds macabre, but it isn't.'

Perhaps the best view from the house takes in the village and the crumbling church. Despite various setbacks, Tim insists that Mindya is recovering, albeit slowly. While certainly boasting a quieter pace of life, there are still things to see and do, and Tim regularly walks his rescue dog Bunny around the neighbourhood, pursued by packs of friendly hounds. More inspiring, perhaps, are the local markets, such as the weekly one in Gorna Oryahovitsa, where he found the sculpture on the balcony.

Having left most of his possessions behind, Tim has spent much of his time in flea markets over the years – something he has done all his life. 'My partner currently lives and works in Kiev,' says Tim. 'We are always foraging for things, scouring the markets, looking for anything that takes our eye. We find things in our respective countries and swap them from

OPPOSITE Two separate pieces of furniture have been brought together and topped with a selection of Bulgarian jars and pots.

house to house, like a cultural exchange. A great example of this is the red and white fabric on the chest in the bedroom, which is typically Ukrainian, while the green wine jar on top is a typically Bulgarian vessel found locally.'

The result is an eclectic mix of objects, enhanced by the retention of classic Bulgarian features. The most striking of these is located in the bedroom: a *jamal*, or stove, which resembles a wardrobe and reaches up to the ceiling. When they moved in, the couple also inherited an old Bulgarian blouse and apron, which now hang on the back of a bedroom door, whose contrasting shade of green – light jade, next to a lime cabinet – remains precisely how they found it. Elsewhere, they have largely filled the place with locally found items.

'The paintings in the single bedroom are mainly of Veliko Tarnovo, the nearby town, and have been collected over the years,' Tim says. 'The old dairy cart – for delivering milk and cheese in the village – came from a neighbour.'

While the majority of objects are foraged from flea markets, Tim also goes hunting in the aforementioned derelict buildings. 'There are lots of these houses in the village, and they're full of broken bits and pieces that I am always reclaiming,' he explains – such as the old white table in the kitchen, along with a sideboard made from two different pieces of furniture.

In a way, this sums up the couple's overall approach: the bringing together of ideas and objects, and making them work – whether it is eclectic with traditional, or contemporary with quintessential. Instead of creating friction, they harmonize.

And so the last word and action is given to the Bulgarians: 'The previous owners love what we've done here,' says Tim. 'They always cry.'

ABOVE AND OPPOSITE Although largely based in Bulgaria ('many houses in the village are similar'), Tim spends much of his time travelling to Ukraine and working in Spain.

Forest foraging

It is a clear November day in Oslo, where broad northern hills cradle the city below and ferries disgorge from the harbour. Out towards the horizon, low and smooth and green, the Oslofjord twists and turns, while across the pretty capital, on the opposing arm of the hills, a giant brontosaurus, otherwise known as Holmenkollen ski jump, lumbers laboriously over the rocks.

It is the weekend, and the natives are out and about, enjoying the fresh air: hiking, cycling, ski-skating. For those just here for the view, a fire burns in a nearby brazier. It is chilly at this time of year, but the hills remain free of snow. You could spend all day here, in fact, quiet and thoughtful and serene.

'Off we go!' calls Heidi Bjørnsdotter Thorvik (see p. 182), wearing a woollen jumper and wellies, a canvas bag strapped to her back.

There are numerous winding trails leading off into the surrounding forest. Heidi walks ahead, brisk and sure-footed. The path is muddy and thick with pine needles. Blue tits and chaffinches slice through the air. It is surprisingly lush and green. In addition to pine, the forest is dominated by spruce and birch. Christmas trees in their natural habitat can be bizarrely disconcerting. They look out of place here, spread across the forest floor, rather than crammed into the corner of someone's sitting room, their branches decorated with tinsel and plastic baubles.

'The Trafalgar Square tree is a gift from Norway, every year since the war,' Heidi explains. 'It's quite sad seeing all those trees left on the street after the holiday. I remember reading about someone in England who took some of these trees and used the wood for some kind of project.'

Not dissimilar, then, to what she's doing now. But before business, comes lunch. She approaches a small clearing. Logs surround a wood and stone pit; Oslo is just visible through the trees. As she builds a fire, Heidi explains that trees are being cut down to enhance the view. The upshot is that she can forage among the felled ones, and doesn't need to damage trees that are thriving.

Lunch consists of sandwiches filled with ham and a sweet brown cheese. These are followed by cake and local apples, washed down with milky coffee from wooden ladles.

'My interest in foraging comes from my parents,' Heidi says. 'My dad was a passionate collector of stones and weird things he found in nature. He once brought a wasps' nest inside that he thought was empty. It wasn't. They started crawling out of the bookshelf.'

After finishing her food, Heidi gazes at the dying fire. 'It's something deep inside of us,' she says.

There is a brief sense of time coming loose at the seams, and then, in one swift action, Heidi is up and on the move again. A knife hangs from her hip and she wields a hatchet in her right hand. Before long, she comes to a length of pine tree. She sets upon it with her axe, chipping away at the bark. It's damp and rotting and comes off easily.

'It's amazing how you can find colours from plants and nature,' she says, holding up a section of orangey-brown bark. 'I dry this, then crush it into a powder, and then use the powder to colour my textiles.'

What she forages today will likely be used on old linen, but she also uses bark as decoration or as a standalone piece for the home. 'As we say in Norway, *å koke suppe på spiker*, which roughly translates as "cook soup on a nail". It means utilizing every resource. The environment has always been important to me when using materials.'

She continues through the forest, dropping further down the hill. In the distance, partly camouflaged by the crisscrossing branches, the long neck of the ski jump rears smoothly upward. After a few metres more, Heidi finds a dead silver birch.

'When it's springtime,' she explains, 'the sap makes it easy to loosen, but now it's quite tight.'

Undeterred, she cuts an incision in the paper-thin layers of bark, and pulls off long tapering strips. The layers darken the deeper she gets. 'The darker brown is better for colour,' she says. 'The outer layer can be used for weaving baskets.'

She demonstrates with three of the strips, neatly braiding them together, the finished article falling silently to the forest floor.

Half an hour more of foraging, then Heidi is back in her car. It is late afternoon as she descends towards the city. On the opposite side of Oslo, the sun drops suddenly behind the hills, burnishing the cold, blue waters. As she swings round a hairpin, the fjord heaves gradually into view, its low and gentle slopes turned the same rusty orange as the bark poking out of her bag.

URBAN

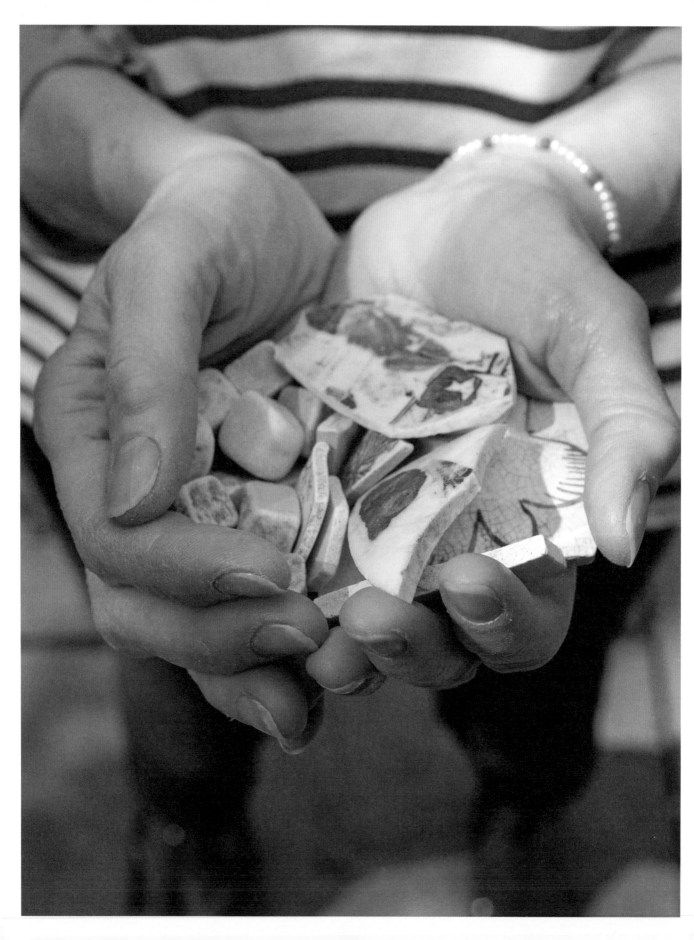

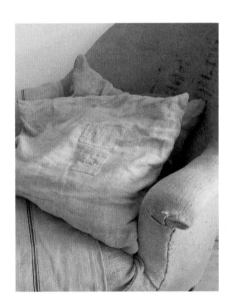

Urban foraging

In theory, urban environments should be giant repositories of foragable objects. With millions of people living side by side, and fads and fashions ever changing, it is a wonder that roadsides aren't overflowing with antiques. In reality, there are laws and systems in place – after all, nobody likes a litterbug. So while you may be lucky enough to spot the occasional piece of furniture outside someone's front door, if you really want access to a hoard of unwanted objects, the likelihood is that you'll need to be a little bit savvier.

Dumps, skips, garage sales, flea markets, charity shops: these are the kinds of places where urban foragers can find things. In addition, there are a wealth of websites where people want to offload their possessions – often for free. All you have to do is collect them. Being part of Scandinavia, it goes without saying that Norway is exceptionally clean and tidy, and Marianne Vigtel Hølland (Slow Design; p. 238) has found a great number of extraordinary objects by employing such simple online methods.

Of course, not all cities are barren concrete jungles. Many urban centres boast parks, woods and hillsides, and several foragers in this chapter combine walking the dog with collecting things for the home. Conversely, Ragnhild Wik (Potter's Studio; p. 246) finds plenty of natural objects on Oslo's streets, sometimes tossed into hedgerows.

Indeed, if you look hard enough, beyond the inevitable filth and rubbish, the city might contain some truly remarkable things. When it comes to mudlarking, for example, foragers must literally dig a little deeper. With the aid of a permit and a pair of latex gloves, Caroline and Beth (Mudlarking; p. 224) do just that, sifting through the mud and sand of the River Thames, peeling back the centuries as they go.

Just like cities themselves, opportunities for urban foraging are extremely rich and varied. It may be more demanding than in other places, requiring added time and effort, but the rewards are invariably worth it.

Georgian Townhouse

Bath, UK

'God, I've got a load of old rubbish, haven't I?' So says Jude Wisdom, describing her extraordinary home in the Georgian town of Bath in Somerset, in southwest England.

'I've always loved rustic,' she adds. 'The great thing about it is that if you are disorganized, or a bit mad, it doesn't matter. You don't have to live up to anything. Because the house isn't pristine, it fits in with who we are as a family.' Which roughly translates as a home – and a family – with bags of personality.

Originally from Essex, Jude attended art college in nearby Corsham in the 1980s. She remained in the area, doing illustrations for magazines, and eventually writing and illustrating her own children's books. She met her husband, Luther, at Glastonbury Festival, and they have a son and two daughters together.

'I've always foraged,' she says. 'When I went to college, my mother was aghast, because she sent me off drawing pictures of hippos. Within two years I'd shaved my hair off and was sticking Rizla packets onto the wall. My friend and I used to go the Bath flea market and buy things like pith helmets. I bought a moose's head once. We spent our student grants on tat, basically, instead of food. Generally, though, foraging was born out of necessity. We also drew on our walls to pretty them up a bit.'

A habit that is also adopted in this home, where the couple have lived since 1994. Located in the quiet 'suburb' of Larkhall, their terraced house didn't require much renovating, aside from knocking through the front room and under the stairs. They plan to eventually take down the lean-to and replace it with something simple and rustic, using corrugated iron – foraged, naturally.

When walking their dog – a cocker spaniel called Hector with long blonde locks worthy of a cartoon prince – they often pick things up for the home. 'We forage as a family,' Jude says. 'We go over Woolley to Upper Swainswick, literally five minutes' walk from here. It's the last valley

ABOVE The orange voodoo doll on the desk was made by the couple's daughter Daisy. **OPPOSITE** An old French daybed from a flea market.

in the Cotswolds, very *Cider with Rosie*. There's sheep's wool, sheep skulls, anything sheep-related – and lots of branches. There's one in the front room with this gorgeous yellow on it. It's not lichen – it's probably a disease – but it looks really nice.'

On the whole, plants are preferable to skulls – as are shells, driftwood, bird's nests, stones and pebbles, and feathers found in hedgerows. 'There's a dell in the valley where moss grows, near the roadside,' Jude says. 'The dog has a drink, I grab some moss – happy days. Many of the shells come from Dartmouth, where a cove spews them out with holes in them.'

In addition to foraging outdoors, Jude regularly visits the flea market with her eldest daughter, Daisy. 'We go to the market on a Saturday, have a cup of tea and go see my friend Dawn, who runs The Curious Flea,' she says.

ABOVE Some red string has been tied around a stick and nailed to the wall. The ivy has been there for several years; a large branch snakes along the stairwell.

'We'll usually buy something. It won't be much – maybe just a fiver – but it will be something really lovely.'

Such as the washed-up coral in the sitting room, or the centuries-old French documents, their yellowish paper curled and crinkled. Charity shops are another good place for finding unusual objects: the ship on the mantelpiece, for instance, purchased from the Women's Aid shop, or the homemade bow and arrow bought for 50p. Skips and pavements have also contributed their fair share of bounty over the years, 'the more old and beaten up, the better'.

This description could be applied to the green crate at the top of the stairs or the faded sampler on the wall, not to mention the chair in the bathroom, the large desk in the bedroom, a rack for pots and colanders or the strip of rug fixed to a shelf in the front room. A poster featuring two mirrored heads posed a trickier problem. Jude and Luther were on holiday in Paris when she spotted it by a patisserie in Saint-Germain.

'I had to take it off the wall and shove it under my jumper,' Luther remembers. ' People were looking at me. Meanwhile, Jude had walked off somewhere.'

Jude runs her finger along a shelf, inspecting the smear of dust on its tip. Normally, she likes to keep the house dark and cosy, creating an intimate space that could be 'anywhere in the world'. The shutters in the front room were bought at Frome market and screwed in by Luther. 'To keep the light out, obviously,' she jokes. 'I like living in a hovel.'

'Hovel' is perhaps inaccurate – there is nothing squalid about their home. It is one of great warmth and character, entirely personal to the Wisdom family. It couldn't, in fact, be anywhere else.

ABOVE In the bathroom is a soap dish from a junk shop in Cyprus. **OPPOSITE** A large desk from a school was found on the street, and it is now used for storing art supplies.

Locksmith's House

Vienne, France

Justine Cook, together with her husband and son, has a house in central France, surrounded by hills and forest. However, that is all she's willing to reveal of the location. The area remains relatively untouched, and, quite understandably, she would like to keep it that way. Similarly, she likes to maintain a certain authenticity in her home. 'We're leaving it as it is,' she explains, referring also to her husband and collaborator, David.

'It's the old locksmith's house, built in the grounds of an abbey in around 1850,' Justine adds. 'It had been in the same family ever since, until we bought it about a year ago. We've since stripped it back, leaving the bones of the house, celebrating the building itself. We're not trying to modernize it in any way, apart from introducing hot water and decent electrics.'

The walls are a great example of this respectful approach. Where possible, the couple have tried to retain the original paintwork, while being careful not to compromise. 'The dining room was quite spooky, painted black in the centre,' she says. 'We wanted to keep beautiful bits of paint, but the room needed to be lighter – and to not give people a migraine.'

ABOVE AND LEFT The mirrors on the mantelpiece were found in the house. The taxidermy ducklings are from a *brocante*; the photograph is of a previous member of the household.

Justine and David painted over the beams, which had been painted to look like wood in a misguided attempt at scumbling. The result of their hard work is both homely and theatrical – hardly surprising, given that Justine is an installation artist. This is something that also ties in with her foraging.

'I've always foraged, always collected things,' she says. 'In fact, the first job I did when I set up an art studio was a project called Rag & Bone, along with another artist. We realized that we both foraged. We called it "gutter botany" – bits of rust from the street, skip furniture.'

The couple rarely buy anything new and often visit the local *brocante*. The home is filled with skip finds and inherited objects, such as the day bed in the second bedroom, which Justine found in a French *dechetterie*, or dump. 'I forage because I find beauty in discarded objects,' she says. 'Throwing things away is such a waste. We once found a bedhead in a hedge, rotting away.

We just shook it off and painted it. I enjoy that process, repurposing things you find and making them beautiful again.'

Since moving in, foraging has never been so easy, as a large share of the objects have come from within the house itself. 'When we bought it, we asked the owner to leave behind anything she no longer wanted,' Justine remembers.

This included a cross. David collects religious iconography, and had spotted it in a cupboard during their first visit to the house. Hoping to find it again when they moved in, he discovered that it had been sold. Then, several weeks later, he found it at the flea market, identifying it by a tell-tale chip. 'He paid more than he should have done,' Justine says, 'just to bring it back to the house.'

ABOVE AND OPPOSITE 'We collect apothecary pieces,' Justine explains. 'Some of the crockery was found in the house itself, or else in *brocantes*.'

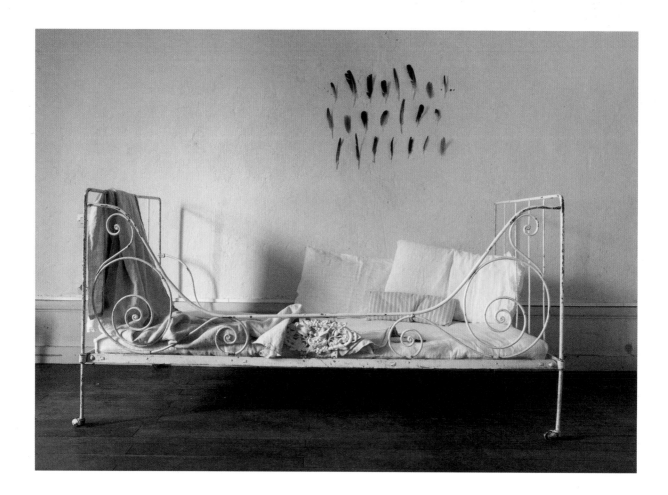

Along with a key safe, crockery, photographs, a shoe, furniture, mirrors and linens – to name a few items found in the house – perhaps the most remarkable discovery was the military uniforms, which date from the First World War.

'One day, after moving some furniture, a tiny piece of paper floated past,' Justine says. 'It was the man's obituary. We were able to trace the uniforms, discovering that he had been a guard outside the Palais-Royal, and that he'd won a medal of honour. It's been very interesting to map the family's history in the house.'

Plenty of objects have been foraged from outside, too, such as honeysuckle, violets – and birds' wings. 'I collect wings and dead birds,' Justine admits. In a curious twist, it transpires that the local community had a habit of putting bones in the walls of their homes. The couple are unsure of the precise reasons for this, but suspect it was to ward off evil spirits or witches.

Meanwhile, a wall in the second bedroom is dedicated to feathers, all collected from around the house and abbey, and stuck there with fine pins. They are mostly from carrion crows, pigeons and mallards. 'They're not all pretty,' Justine says, 'but they go up.'

There are also several branches in the dining room, foraged from a nearby orchard. 'I think our foraging looks quite clean,' she adds.

It's more than just clean. In its simple, unassuming approach, the couple's foraging complements the story of the house, while being very much of the present. Somehow, Justine and David have had it both ways: achieving authenticity not only for the house, but for themselves, as well.

ABOVE The day bed beneath Justine's collection of feathers was found at a dump. **OPPOSITE** The headless mannequin is from an old tailor's shop in France.

Mudlarking

Chelsea Embankment has an easy, slightly forbidding, charm. Built in 1874, it transformed the riverside, and features two of London's most famous bridges: Albert and Battersea. On this late April day, the sun is shining after a week of bad weather, and petals gather in small mounds along the roadside. Like any metropolis, London has its sleepless soundtrack: aeroplanes, traffic, sirens, people. Despite its illustrious history, the Embankment is not immune – far from it, in fact – although it does possess at least one unlikely advantage: the River Thames.

'It's so calming down here,' says Caroline, overturning a stone with a flick of her brightly coloured boot. Finding nothing of interest, she moves on. Behind her lies the Albert Bridge, beneath which a long line of barges and tugboats bob. Across the narrow brown river, to the south, glass-fronted offices rise above the bank. Yet there aren't any likeminded office workers outside, sifting through the mud, sand and stone, doing nothing less than foraging for the footprint of humanity. Perhaps they are just waiting until lunchtime.

'I've found something,' says Caroline.

It's a sherd of blue and white pottery, most likely Georgian or Victorian. About the size of a ten-pence coin, it appears to show a man holding an umbrella. Pleased with her find, and donning a pair of white latex gloves, she drops it into a sealable bag. The hunt continues.

This stretch of river is known as the Tideway, and the water can rise and fall up to 7 m (30 ft) or more. This means that the banks – and what they contain – are ever changing. All sorts of things turn up, some admittedly more exciting than others. So far today there has been a broken pair of yellow-handled pliers, a green bottle cap, bits of glass worn smooth by the tides, half an oyster shell, a blue balloon, a clothes horse, two (broken) bike locks, a pink button, a vape tank and a girl's bicycle.

'I sometimes find credit cards and phones,' says Caroline. 'Lost or thrown away, I don't know. I see a lot of bones, too, though that's more in the east, around Wapping, where butchers used to throw them in the river. I don't pick them up. I also see lots of glass, pottery and nails. A friend of mine looks for prehistoric tools, but that's too subtle for me. Things have to be pretty! Sometimes, on a beautiful day like this, it's like going to the beach.'

The river's history is far longer and more convoluted than the Embankment's. It has borne witness to Neolithic people, early Britons, Romans, Anglo-Saxons, Normans, all the way through to us. Countless secrets lie beneath its surface.

And it's surprisingly easy to gain access to them. All you need is a permit. For foragers like Caroline and her friend Beth – 'just two Chelsea ladies mudlarking' – the Port of London Authority offers a standard foreshore permit, costing £77 and good for three years, which allows the holder to dig to a depth of 7.5 cm (3 in.)

'I did an Airbnb experience two years ago and we went mudlarking,' Caroline explains. 'I thought it was great, and wanted to do it again. It's just a bit of fun, a nice outing. I only go out about once a month.'

More serious people – the sort bearing spades and metal detectors – join the Thames Mudlark Society and dig down to 1.2 m (4 ft). 'Some people are incredible experts,' says Beth. 'They find amazing things.'

Some of these finds include fossils, Roman artefacts, flint hand axes, old padlocks, jewelry … the list goes on. 'I discovered a whole sugar bowl lid, early 18th century, and I find lots of beautiful clay pipes,' she adds.

Might someone make their fortune mudlarking on the Thames? 'Maybe, but there's more interest in historic things. You start seeing more over time. People have an eye for a particular thing, and it's interesting what they gravitate towards. For me, it's like meditation. It's very restful, it takes you out of yourself.'

The water, while murky and uninviting, laps gently against the shore, producing an eerie peace and quiet made all the more unreal by the immediate proximity of the city. Beneath Battersea Bridge, where a cool breeze churns, Caroline and Beth strike it lucky.

'Bridges are good places,' Beth says. 'They catch things.' More blue and white sherds are added to the collection. 'When you find people, houses, glimpses of life from that time, it's magical. And they look very nice in a bowl.'

As the two friends search among the pile of stones, a pair of nesting geese observe them from a barge.

'Look at this,' says Caroline.

It's a stone of some kind, shaped like the cap of a toadstool, and decorated with stripes. She drops it in her bag. The geese hiss. It's time to leave, before the tide comes rolling in.

On the way back to the stairwell, an object pokes through the sand, promising untold riches and fame. It is a tape measure. Perhaps its time just hasn't come. Perhaps this very same tape measure will inspire in future mudlarkers as much awe and wonder as Neolithic tools do in us. Whatever happens, the Thames will flow on by, and its treasures will only increase.

Provençal Townhouse

L'Isle-sur-la-Sorgue, France

The measure of a good mirror usually boils down to one essential thing: the clarity (which isn't to say accuracy) of its reflection. Nothing so literal-minded for Bénédicte Leuwers, however. 'The less I can see, the better,' she says.

This may seem perverse, until you realize that it's the object itself that excites her, its inherent 'poetry'. Admiring one in particular, its surface scratched and bruised, flaked like silver lichen, the aesthetic appeal, if nothing else, soon becomes crystal-clear.

L'Isle-sur-la-Sorgue is a pretty town in southern France, famous for its markets and antiques – the perfect sort of place for someone who likes nothing more than scouring flea markets for unexpected treasures. 'I have walked around markets like this since I was a child,' she says. 'I love old and dirty things.'

Somehow – perhaps because of her obvious passion, or perhaps for the simple reason that she is French – Bénédicte manages to make ' old and dirty' sound impossibly romantic.

In order to find these old and dirty things, she often swoops in at the end of the day, when the traders are packing up (and likely rather tired and defenceless) to rummage through the boxes. On one such occasion, a stallholder was covering her wares with some tattered old curtains. Bénédicte immediately wanted them. 'The woman thought I was crazy,' she says. The curtains now hang in the spare bedroom.

A fashion stylist once upon a time, Bénédicte ended up doing set design for the photoshoots. People became interested in her work, and soon she was an interior designer. Currently, she is a restaurant owner. This suggests a restless character, but perhaps 'curious' is more accurate. She has travelled a lot for work, taking inspiration from all over the world – along with the foraged objects now dotted about the house.

All of these influences have resulted in a lively, kinetic design – although Bénédicte might quibble with the term 'design'. Indeed, as a concept, design is antithetical to what foraging stands for. 'I don't plan it out,' she insists. 'It takes time, slowly building, one thing leading to another.'

OPPOSITE The chaise longue has been stripped of its cover, revealing an inked stamp on the linen underlayer; the cushions are patchwork.

And yet there is a pleasing mutability about the place, something that goes hand in hand with Bénédicte's passion for foraging. 'Passing an object to someone else,' she explains, 'passing on the beauty, being able to let go and allow someone else to enjoy it.'

In other words, interiors don't have to be static. You can change them whenever you want, and foraging is an excellent way of doing this. It goes without saying that some of the objects on display will already have moved on – which isn't to say that one has to be unsentimental. There are things in the house that Bénédicte has had since her twenties (she's now in her fifties).

One of her most cherished treasures is the large mirror hanging in the sitting room. Bits have broken off it each time she has moved, and she enjoys the fact that the object has aged alongside her. 'I love broken things,' she says (again, impossibly romantic).

An example is the chipped crockery stored in a cupboard in the hallway. The plates and bowls have been arranged in a deceptively haphazard fashion. There was no forethought or planning, she just threw them all together and it worked.

The kitchen began in a similar vein, all because of a yellow plate, which hangs on the wall like some sort of religious icon. Its colour inspired the entire scheme of the room. But it is the central pendant light that makes the room. Bénédicte makes the lampshades herself, using damaged fabrics, and takes pleasure in making something beautiful out of what others might consider filthy old rags. Incidentally, the fridge has been wallpapered over. 'You can't cover the oven,' she says, with a hint of regret.

ABOVE French pottery, dried herbs and bits of coral adorn the shelves in the kitchen. **OPPOSITE** The fabric pendant light 'makes the room'.

There are also bunches of dried herbs on the kitchen shelves: bay leaves, thyme, rosemary, all picked nearby. For Bénédicte, herbs and flowers are more beautiful when dried than when they are alive and still growing in the ground.

Examples of this mild obsession are found throughout the house: six long stalks pulled from the side of a road, spilling out of a rusty can; a single white stem, rising out of a fat clay jug; a chain of carob fruit encircling a small metal ring; golden shimmering flowers on a marble mantelpiece. 'Metal plants and dead plants are OK,' she jokes. They are longer-lasting, too.

Plants aside, most of the objects in the house are from the 19th century. Bénédicte likes things that tell a story, such as the green table in the downstairs living area. It was put together with different pieces, and speaks of a collaborative effort, of 'folk art', the spirit of which has much in common with foraging.

Other objects tell more personal stories, like the wooden arm in the spare bedroom.

Bénédicte wanted to give it life again, so now it takes centre stage on the fireplace, joined by a stuffed bird and a pale frond of coral. 'It looked lonely,' she says.

'You never know when you might use something,' she adds, summing up her piecemeal approach. That she manages to bring all these disparate elements so seamlessly together is a mark of both her talent and the dynamic nature of foraging.

ABOVE Patched-up fabric found at a flea market has been turned into cushions. **OPPOSITE** Another foraged find, a sieve, has been converted into a lampshade.

Slow Design

Jar, Norway

'Bandy' is a curious blend of ice hockey and field hockey, though its origins lie somewhere between the two, along the frozen fens of East Anglia. While England has since lost touch with its bandy roots, the sport is alive and well in the outskirts of Oslo, directly below the home of Marianne Vigtel Hølland. From such a warm and comfortable vantage point – watching players skate around a football-sized pitch, chasing a rubber ball – the game can appear ferocious, dependent on startling speed and lightning-quick reflexes.

A stark contrast, then, to Marianne's self-described concept of 'slow design'. 'By slow, I mean to let something unfold itself, not to hurry, but to take your time,' she explains.

Something that applies not only to design, but also to how she chooses to live. 'It's something that has emerged as I've grown older,' she continues. 'After having kids, I thought about environmental issues, how we use too much, the pressure to buy new stuff. The wheels are turning faster and faster, and I didn't want to be a part of that.'

Marianne has lived in the house for over 16 years, and it is a living testament to her philosophy, one that has seen her, and her family, battle the elements. Despite this, or perhaps because of it, the house is peaceful and intimate, just the place you want to be as winter draws ever nearer.

The open living area provides the perfect example. The frame above the sofa was originally a large plank of oak that she found near the sea. 'It was very heavy,' she says, 'so I forced my son to help me.'

This involved carrying it several kilometres to their boat. Her husband wasn't best pleased at the time, but soon relented when the framed picture was presented as a gift. In fact, Marianne readily acknowledges his role in tempering such foraging excesses, especially when they're on holiday. 'Only things that fit in our luggage are allowed,' she admits.

Some objects in the house are from childhood, others collected when Marianne was a student, but most things have been built and foraged by the couple since moving in. Besides the frame, there are beautiful pieces of wood – plus shells and stones – scattered liberally throughout the property.

ABOVE The chest originally belonged to a pharmacy and was bought at a garage sale. The wool rug hanging on the wall was made by Marianne. 'The wool is untreated,' she says. 'I like the natural expression of it.'

In addition to beachcombing, Marianne does much of her foraging in forests, flea markets, garage sales and online. A random assortment of found objects includes pebbles along the fireplace, a coat rack fashioned from driftwood, a (vacated) wasp's nest above a bookshelf, oyster shells in a plant pot, a rusty drill bit in a jar on a windowsill, antlers foraged by her dog, Stella ('she works for me'), and a foundational wire mesh on the outside wall.

There is even barbed wire: 'Whenever I see barbed wire in the forest, I pick it up, because quite a few animals get stuck.' This includes Stella, who bears a scar on her belly. 'I can use it for other stuff instead,' Marianne says – such as lamps or wall hangings. 'Because it's rusty, the colour comes off on the fabric when it rains, which is nice. I like destroyed things.'

This is evident elsewhere, too: the exploded armchairs, for example – or, at least, that's how they appear, with the springs and stuffing exposed. 'A shop was redecorating,' she explains. 'The chairs were used in a window display and were going to be thrown away. The staff at the shop didn't think anybody would use them.'

They were wrong, of course, and Marianne got them for nothing. But perhaps the most striking feature is the charred wood. In several rooms, if you looked closely, you would notice that the doors, cupboards, even a sofa base, have been burnt to a literal crisp. She first had the idea when building the outside cabin.

OPPOSITE A paper-thin, blueish-grey wasp's nest sits above a bookshelf. Another example of Marianne's handiwork is the lampshade in the bedroom.

'It's an old technique to protect the wood,' Marianne explains. 'When we were making our furniture, I asked the man who had helped us with the cabin to bring me some of this charred wood. He thought I was crazy, but I love the texture. Some people wouldn't like this,' she adds, peeling blackened flakes off the sofa.

She has made a number of objects by hand, recycling wherever possible. Many are made from wool – given to her by a farmer – and include net curtains, blankets and lampshades. The seating on the outdoor terrace was made using beams foraged from a torn-down barn, and on her bedroom wall hangs a found iron hoop, trailing a piece of fabric.

Some things are made at her workbench, which she found in a garage sale. It belonged to a man who made violins and many of the features are redundant, though by no means unappreciated. Over the years, Marianne has found a number of extraordinary objects both at garage sales and online. Like the workbench,

they have a history, albeit an indirect one, and still carry traces of what makes an inherited object sacred: a connection to the past, coupled with a renewed sense of purpose and meaning.

There is also the practical side of things: if the objects aren't strictly free, they are invariably cheap. The floor of the summerhouse, for example, is from an old stable. After seeing the paint-spattered boards on a website, Marianne drove many kilometres to fetch them, paying a mere 300 kroner (£28) for as much as she wanted: 'I regret not going back for more.'

Fortunately, there's very little else to regret. While ice, sweat and tears are shed down below, inside remains blissfully quiet.

OPPOSITE The boxes (with apples on top of them) were collected from a garage sale. **ABOVE** The brown bottles contain dyes made from bark and onions: 'If you leave them in the sun, the colour gets stronger.'

Potter's Studio

Oslo, Norway

It is autumn in central Oslo. There is a small park nearby,
and a cold wind blows through the trees. Leaves drift past the
windows, gathering in the courtyard below. In the comfort of
her studio, Ragnhild Wik's copper-coloured hair likewise shimmers
and cascades. She has been known to pluck out a strand or two –
strictly for the purposes of her pottery, of course – but for now,
she leaves her hair alone, and instead pours coffee into cups that
she made herself.

The process of making the cups took two weeks, including drying, firing and glazing. Each one is unique and tactile, complete with a small leather strap from which to hang it. 'I don't like strict design,' Ragnhild says. 'It needs to be free and loose, where the soul is.'

Ragnhild was a costume designer before starting work at a porcelain factory. For many years, she designed ceramics on the computer, admiring the craftsmen from afar, and later ran a successful business with friends, before selling her share in 2015. There was something else she wanted to do, something that wouldn't involve meetings, statistics and the management of other people. She wanted to make things with her own hands, to be free and keep things small.

And so here she is: in a pink building with no straight lines. The space is essentially two rooms

ABOVE Ragnhild makes some of her glazes according to an old Russian technique, using milk or yoghurt and made with a pit fire.

– one large area containing much of her finished work, along with a living and kitchen area, and a smaller room at the rear for her studio proper. The building curves round, completing a near semicircle. Its unusual shape provides a pleasing symmetry with Ragnhild's ceramics, something that is also present in the many cracks and holes in the brick wall (the only thing she did was paint it white). 'I like things to have a story,' she says – like the green, bespattered floor.

The previous tenant owned a number of large machines, which, instead of moving outside, he simply painted around, leaving random geometric shapes in the wood. Over a century old, the floor has a shallow channel running through it, rubbed smooth and shiny by countless footsteps. There is a real sense of historic activity, something that feeds directly into Ragnhild's approach to foraging.

Quite a few items were found online, by poring over websites on which people give things away for free. 'I like the patina of old furniture, and the quality,' she says.

Not only does she pick up an interesting piece of furniture, but she also gains a little insight into how other people live, forming a brief but satisfying connection. Her desk was obtained this way, as was the large dining table, which belonged to a family moving house.

'As long as things are durable, you can play with them,' Ragnhild says – which she duly did with her grandmother's table, painting it jet-black. She also gets inspiration from the Salvation Army. After finding some 1960s

ABOVE AND OPPOSITE 'I thought after one or two years I would have done it all, but I've barely started,' Ragnhild says. 'There are infinite possibilities of shape and colour.'

cutlery, she soaked the handles overnight in olive oil, blackening the wood – a straightforward process with a surprisingly sophisticated result.

Looking around, it quickly becomes apparent that there are broken bits of ceramic everywhere. Some have been collected in a big bowl, others used to create elegant works of art, like the Big Bang. Ragnhild doesn't like wasting things, but it's more than that. 'Sometimes I keep them for inspiration,' she says. 'I like turning things into new things. It's exciting to work with.'

A similar spirit can be found in the Japanese art of *kintsugi*, in which fragments of pottery are joined together with a seam of lacquer and gold. As a result, an object can be more attractive broken than when whole. It is not too far-fetched to apply this philosophy to foraging. In many cases, what people consider ugly and damaged is actually quite the opposite, if only they could view it slightly differently, or had the tools and experience necessary to make the misunderstood object beautiful again.

Autumn is a great time for a different sort of foraging. Scattered throughout the studio are leaves, berries, stones and herbs. 'The herbs were thrown away, so I just picked them up,' Ragnhild explains. Very simple, entirely free, yet they almost make the room.

Of her pottery, she adds, 'I work very intuitively, and love to make things by hand. It is always exciting when you're experimenting. Sometimes it works, sometimes it doesn't.'

The same goes for the freewheeling nature of foraging. And in this particular instance, there's certainly no shortage of soul.

ABOVE AND OPPOSITE 'I like new beginnings and things that have a story,' Ragnhild says. 'Recycling is a way to experience that all the time.'

Directory

We would like to thank Mike Sajnoski – husband/*beau-frère* – for his tireless support and superlative post-production skills; Deborah Beau, without whom this book wouldn't exist, sitting round the (foraged) kitchen table, helping conceive of the idea and carrying out essential research; and also Poppy – daughter/niece – for her extraordinary patience and understanding during her mother's long absences.

And thank you, of course, to every person featured in this book – and plenty of others besides – who welcomed us into their incredible homes and were unfailingly kind and generous, even when there were four of us to deal with. Not to mention the laughs: two simultaneous meals; an impenetrable rental car; the joyous mayhem of a pan-Australia odyssey; an electric kettle burnt on a hot stove – all of it fuelled by excellent food and wine. It would take too long to name you individually, but we hope you know just how special you've made this experience for us.

Finally, we would like to thank Elain McAlpine and Lucas Dietrich, and the whole team at Thames & Hudson, who have done a remarkable job in helping us realize this book, of which we are excessively proud.

Joanna & Ollie x

To our mother, or else she'd never forgive us

ON THE COVER Front A cottage in Dorset, UK **Back, clockwise from top left** A converted church in Boonah, Australia; gathering seaweed in Lyme Regis, Dorset; foraged finds on the wall of a rural cottage in Dorset; wreath-making in Australia